COLONIAL CROSSFIRE

Welsh Experiences from Both Sides
of the Falklands / Malvinas War

COLONIAL CROSSFIRE

Welsh Experiences from Both Sides of the Falklands/Malvinas War

Ioan Roberts

Translated by
John Howard Jones
and **Malcolm Evans**

Gwasg Carreg Gwalch

First published in Welsh in 2003 as *Rhyfel Ni* ('Our War')
© text: Ioan Roberts
© English translation: John Howard Jones and Malcolm Evans
© publication: Gwasg Carreg Gwalch

ISBN: 978-1-84527-890-8
ebook ISBN: 978-1-84524-478-1

CYNGOR LLYFRAU CYMRU
BOOKS COUNCIL of WALES

Published with the financial support of the Books Council of Wales

Cover design: Lynwen Jones
Maps: Ken Gruffydd

Published by Gwasg Carreg Gwalch,
12 Iard yr Orsaf, Llanrwst, Dyffryn Conwy, Cymru LL26 0EH.
Tel: 01492 642031
email: llyfrau@carreg-gwalch.cymru
website: www.carreg-gwalch.cymru

Printed and published in Wales

CONTENTS

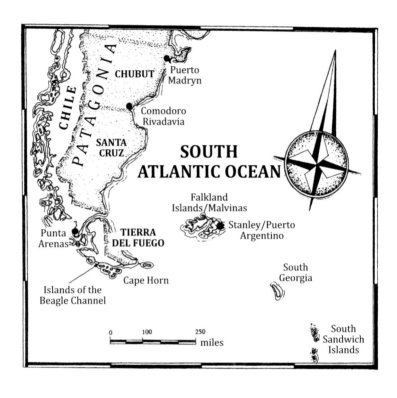

CHILE

PATAGONIA

CHUBUT

Puerto
Madryn

Comodoro
Rivadavia

SANTA
CRUZ

SOUTH
ATLANTIC OCEAN

Falkland
Islands/Malvinas

Stanley/Puerto
Argentino

Punta
Arenas

TIERRA
DEL FUEGO

South
Georgia

Cape Horn

Islands of the
Beagle Channel

South
Sandwich
Islands

0   100   250
miles

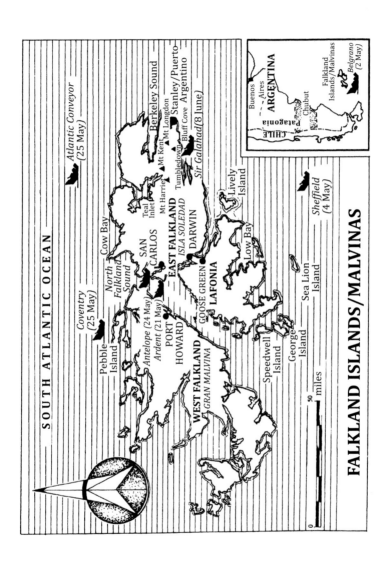

FALKLAND ISLANDS/MALVINAS

SOUTH ATLANTIC OCEAN

Atlantic Conveyor (25 May)

Coventry (25 May)

Pebble Island

North Falkland Sound

Cow Bay

Berkeley Sound

Teal Inlet

SAN CARLOS

Mt Kent

Mt Longdon

Stanley/Puerto Argentino

Mt Harriet

Tumbledown

Bluff Cove

Sir Galahad (8 June)

EAST FALKLAND

ISLA SOLEDAD

DARWIN

Lively Island

Antelope (24 May)

Ardent (21 May)

PORT HOWARD

GOOSE GREEN

LAFONIA

Low Bay

WEST FALKLAND

GRAN MALVINA

Speedwell Island

George Island

Sea Lion Island

Sheffield (4 May)

miles

50

CHILE

Patagonia

ARGENTINA

Buenos Aires

Chubut

Falkland Islands/Malvinas

Belgrano (2 May)

7

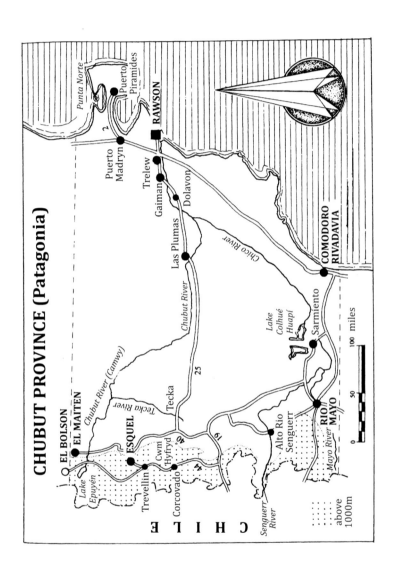

CHUBUT PROVINCE (Patagonia)

PREFACE (2022)

This translation of *Rhyfel Ni* ('Our War'), first published in Welsh in 2003, marks the 40th anniversary of the Falklands/Malvinas conflict and honours the book's author, Ioan Roberts, who died in January 2019. A Spanish translation is also in progress. This is an oral history which captures the brutality of the fighting and its traumatic legacy for combatants, along with the grief of bereaved parents and loved ones. It expresses the particular pain felt in Y Wladfa, the part of Patagonia where the first European settlers were Welsh migrants whose language and culture persists among their descendants today, supported by strong links with 'yr Hen Wlad' (the Old Country, Wales).

Y Wladfa's story is one of a flight to freedom and self-determination from English cultural and religious domination at home. Through this other 'kith and kin' narrative, very different from the one used to justify the dispatch of the UK's Task Force to the South Atlantic, the tragic absurdity of the late colonial conflict Jorge Luis Borges famously compared to two bald men fighting over a comb was, as Ioan Roberts shows, compounded for British Welsh and Patagonian Welsh combatants, who found themselves on opposite sides fighting each other. At the end of it the Royal Navy repatriated many of the Argentinian prisoners of war to Puerto Madryn in Y Wladfa, where the clipper *Mimosa*, sailing from Liverpool, landed the first group of Welsh settlers in 1865.

Twenty years after the conflict, Ioan Roberts tracked down and recorded the testimony of men and women of Welsh origin or descent on both sides. From these interviews emerged a document of compassion and unflinching realism, with no glorification of war or sanitizing of violence and suffering through military jargon or operational euphemism. This echoes modern Welsh literary and cultural tradition, deeply etched with the horrors of war and radically different in tone from the conservative and imperial Britishness one might associate with Kipling, Churchill, or 'Rule Britannia'.

Or indeed with Margaret Thatcher, who in 1982 rallied the 'waverers and the fainthearts' in her country to acknowledge the full glory of the Falklands triumph:

> The people who thought that Britain could no longer seize the initiative for herself. The people who thought we could no longer do the great things which we once did. Those who believed that our decline was irreversible – that we could never again be what we were . . . that Britain was no longer the nation that had built an empire and ruled a quarter of the world. Well they were wrong. The lesson of the Falklands is that Britain has not changed and that this nation still has those sterling qualities that shine through our history.

Another two decades on, these words echo through subsequent British military adventuring, an intensifying nationalism and insularity that came to a head with Brexit, costume drama nostalgia for the English country house and empire, along with emerging dreams of an Empire 2.0 in which severed ties with and responsibilities to Europe are replaced by a revitalized British Commonwealth of nations. All this resonating behind current conservative challenges to so-called 'woke' thinking with its distaste for jingoistic nationalism and its emphasis on diversity, equality, inclusion and open-mindedness - along with practical redress for the past evils of slavery and colonialism.

Cultural historians open to the other side of that debate also see the Falklands/Malvinas war as an important landmark in the development of a more combative English nationalism. Sathnam Sanghera, who quotes the words of Margaret Thatcher reproduced above (2021, p.110) and Fintan O'Toole (2018), for example, both offer fascinating snapshots of the South Atlantic conflict in relation to prior and subsequent perceptions of Britain and its role in the world. The continuing conversations around what the political right, with its fondness for military metaphors, likes to call this 'culture war', makes *Rhyfel Ni*, if anything, even more relevant in the current climate than it was at the time of its publication, particularly for a wider Anglophone and international audience. Our title, *Colonial Crossfire*, reflects this expansion of the context, which may be helped by the happy historical accident that the 'Welsh' label happens to derive from the Anglo-Saxon invader's word for 'stranger' or 'foreigner'. Apart from those blessed with one of those exceptionalist identities, chosen by god or some form of historical destiny, we are all foreigners and in that sense, perhaps, 'Welsh' as well, content to be 'other' rather than adamantly special and singled out. It is a rich plurality of identities. In the words of the historian Gwyn Alf Williams: "If you feel Welsh, you are Welsh". In the language we have three emotionally resonant and ultimately untranslatable words for this: Cynefin. Croeso. Heddwch.

But colonial myths may also flourish on the idea of being victimized, passed over or marked by some historical slight. Fintan O'Toole shows how Brexit culture, for example, was infused not only with a national exceptionalism but a 'strange sense of imaginary oppression' reflecting 'a nation that feels sorry for itself' (2018, pp. xvii, 1). This mixture of specialness and what O'Toole calls 'tender regard for our terribly wronged selves' is nowhere more clearly expressed than in the heartbreakingly melancholy strains of England's national football anthem 'Three Lions'. Geraldine Lublin, who first introduced us, the translators of this book, to Ioan Roberts and who makes an appearance in *Rhyfel Ni* as a young Welsh-speaking Argentinian, has shown since then, in her work on Welsh Patagonia (2017), that Y Wladfa too was an example of settler colonialism, perhaps unwittingly for the early Welsh migrants in flight from their own colonial overlords. As such it supported Argentina's land claims and subsequently its genocidal 'desert campaign' waged against Patagonia's indigenous peoples, the nomadic strangers, the inconvenient foreign bodies *in situ*. These contradictions, which add another dimension to the narrative, are also hinted at occasionally in the chapters that follow.

In his Introduction, Ioan Roberts writes that he has neither the credentials nor the wish to be a military historian, only to record the experiences and reflections of those affected directly by the war, and of their families and communities. What follows is a polyphony of voices that invites readers to make up their own minds. We extend these voices here to a wider audience, in dark days again of empires at war, in the spirit of Rebecca Solnit's glimpses of light in the darkness (2016, p.xiv), the recognition that real changes can begin with changing the story, and that 'every conflict is in part a battle over the story we tell, or who tells and who is heard'.

Malcolm Evans
John Howard Jones
March 2022

Acknowledgments: This translation is dedicated to the memory of Ioan Roberts, in appreciation of an extraordinary talent expressed tirelessly across a rich body of work written and broadcast in Welsh and in English. With thanks beyond measure for his interest and kindness. We thank again all the contributors he interviewed and generously acknowledged for sharing their experience of events no one, in Wales or Y Wladfa, would ever want to face again. Our warmest thanks also go out also to Alwena Roberts, Myrddin ap Dafydd, Geraldine Lublin, Russell Isaac, Ximena Tobi, Patricio Delfosse, Nadine Laporte, Guillermo Williams, Fabio Trevor Gonzales, Mic Dixon, David Collins, Isabel Cartwright and Ellis Brooks.

INTRODUCTION

It is midnight at the *Tavarn Las* pub, still very early in a country where anyone with any sense has been asleep all afternoon. That's why the place is empty apart from the barman and two old chaps from the Llŷn Peninsula, Dafydd M. Jones, who's on holiday in the area, and myself. Dafydd isn't in the best of moods, having had his leg bitten a few hours earlier by a black and white mongrel called Robat. But just as we are deciding to head back to the *Tŷ Gwyn* guest house, they start to arrive from the restaurant in Michael D. Jones Street, two or three young people at first , then by the dozen until the *Tavarn Las* is suddenly crowded. All the chatter is in Welsh, but if you listen carefully enough you will hear two dialects - Llŷn and Patagonia. Half the group are Urdd (National Voluntary Youth Organisation of Wales) members from Llanuwchlyn, and the other half are young locals from Gaiman, inspired by the recent revival of interest in the Welsh language in Y Wladfa (the Welsh communities of the Chubut Valley). In no time the Tavarn Las is one great wave of song, with everyone except the barman, Dafydd and myself singing 'Pan Ddaw Yfory', 'Calon Lân', and 'Yma o Hyd' - not typical pub roaring either but measured and in harmony.

You could pontificate for a month of Sundays about Y Wladfa. Did it make sense for the early Welsh migrants to come here? Were they tricked? Do we over-romanticize the place? Is there a future for the Welsh language here? But you would have to be dreadfully cynical not to feel some kind of thrill in your heart on a night like this in Gaiman, with the spirit and enthusiasm of young people from Chubut and Meirioneth bridging five generations and seven thousand miles. Given my reason for visiting, I couldn't help but reflect that if this happy crew had been here twenty years earlier some of them might have been trying to kill each other on the bleak pieces of land six hundred miles offshore from the *Tavarn Las*, to decide whether those islands should be called the Falklands or the Malvinas.

When soldiers from Wales were fighting and dying on the islands in 1982 in a war over the rights of people there who were being described in Britain as 'kith and kin', it is more than likely that the number of Welsh speakers in Patagonia, in the land of the 'enemy', outnumbered the entire population of the Falklands. Those Welsh speakers were as convinced as any other Argentinian that the Malvinas belonged to Argentina, with most of them, at the onset at least, in support of the attempt to re-establish sovereignty over the islands by force. And yes, some descendants of the Welsh people who established Y Wladfa were fighting on the islands against a British army which included many young men from the 'Hen Wlad', the old country, Wales.

Being aware of these connections would not have affected the attitudes of those caught up in battle: your antagonist being perhaps a distant cousin is the last thing on your mind if the choice is between killing and being killed. And there was no place for the Welsh perspective in the quarrels between Britain and Argentina leading up to the war. In the eyes of Britain, the Argentinians had seized another country's territory by force, against both international law and the wishes of the people who had lived on the islands for generations. From the Argentinian standpoint, this was only to right a wrong that happened a century and a half earlier, when Britain stole the Malvinas by military force from their vulnerable young nation. But for some people, in Wales and in Patagonia, the connection between these two communities, almost as old as the one between England and the Falklands, put a different light on the war. It wasn't as simple for Welsh people to accept a mindset like that of *The Sun*, which portrayed the 'Argies' as some kind of sub-humans, knowing that those people might include friends and relatives from Y Wladfa. There was also a good chance that many people in Y Wladfa realized that Margaret Thatcher did not represent the opinion of the whole population of Wales – in spite of a letter published in *Y Cymro* at the time written by someone from Y Wladfa accusing Welsh soldiers of supporting the 'thieving and rapacious British colonial war.'

I was working at the time as editor of *Y Dydd*, in the newsroom of HTV in Pontcanna, Cardiff. The programme was coming to the end of its lifespan, part of the restructuring associated the arrival of S4C. Unlike the brief for news programmes on the new channel, which were to attend to matters concerning 'Wales, Britain and the world', Wales alone was our usual focus at that time. But suddenly, just before our scheduled disappearance, here we were in the middle not only of the world's biggest story, but also one with a specifically Welsh angle to it.

First of all, the Welsh were suffering the heaviest casualties. The single biggest disaster of the war on the British side was the attack on the *Sir Galahad*, where 33 members of the Welsh Guards were killed. On another ship, *HMS Ardent*, Raymond Roberts from Llanberis lost his life. In an interview on *Y Dydd* his parents were asked about their reaction to the news. His father answered, through his tears, that they thought of the parents of the hundreds of young Argentinians who died when the *General Belgrano* was sunk. That, for me, was one of the most moving and painful observations of the whole war. Mr and Mrs Roberts have the last word in this book.

As with all the recent wars there was, at that time, debate

about the responsibilities of journalists. Should they be backing 'our boys' come what may, like *The Sun* and most of the London tabloids, or trying to report the truth despite the efforts of the authorities to control everything seen or heard from the battlefield? Most broadcasters would insist on their objectivity, but there is always a danger that reporters who depend on the military to get their job done will become pretty much part of that machine. The 'our boys' element is never far away. What complicated matters, for Welsh reporting on the Falklands/Malvinas war, was that 'our boys' were fighting on both sides.

Y Dydd decided to break new ground by sending a journalist to Patagonia during the war to report on the experiences of the Welsh community there. It happened that we had a young reporter on our staff who had lived in Y Wladfa and was fluent in Spanish. Russell Isaac got the opportunity to go back to be among his friends and contemporaries there, also contemporaries of the young Argentinians who were on the Malvinas. But when his reports started to come back they caused a stir among the upper echelons of HTV. The result being, as we shall see in Chapter 14, that the first (and last) war correspondent of *Y Dydd* was back at his desk in Pontcanna by the time the real war had started.

During the war and in subsequent months there were a number of stories around in which Welsh speakers on both sides met each other on the battlefield. Nearly all these, as far as I can see, were products of the imagination. The most romantic story in circulation, was of a Welsh nurse in Port Stanley meeting a young soldier from Y Wladfa when they were both on their knees in church, reciting The Lord's Prayer in Welsh. This story too had been exaggerated, but it wasn't completely without foundation.

In 1990, while filming at the Eisteddfod of Y Wladfa in Trelew for the programme *Hel Straeon*, I was introduced to a young man who had just been conducting a choir on stage. His name was Milton Rhys and he was the soldier who met the nurse. The main flaw in the story was that neither spoke more than a few words of Welsh, though they were both proud of their Welsh heritage, blood being thicker than water. The recollections of Milton Rhys and Bronwen Williams appear in the third and fourth chapters.

During that trip to Y Wladfa I heard about the mental anguish many went through during the war, torn between their adopted homeland and ancestral home, their 'Hen Wlad'. The cruelest irony for the people of Y Wladfa was that it was to Puerto Madryn, where the first Welsh landed on the *Mimosa* in 1865, that the thousands of prisoners of war were taken for repatriation at the end of the fighting 117 years later.

Though much had been written and broadcast about the war I was conscious that nothing had been put on record specifically about the Welsh related experiences on both sides. This book is an attempt to fill that gap. It came to be partly through an unexpected opportunity in 2002 to work with Tweli Griffiths, a friend and colleague since the time of *Y Dydd*, on a programme made by the team from *Y Byd ar Bedwar* marking the twentieth anniversary of the war. Following on from that work, with the encouragement of Myrddin ap Dafydd from the publishers Gwasg Carreg Gwalch, a successful application was made to the Books Council of Wales for a commission that allowed me to go back to Y Wladfa in the autumn of 2002 to carry out the additional research for this book.

I have neither the credentials nor the wish to be a military historian. The turbulent months of 1982 have been documented by many of those already. Although the first two chapters do set some of the historical context for what follows, this is not an analysis of the war but records the experiences of individuals on both sides whose lives were affected more or less directly by it. The first chapters deal mainly with the experiences of soldiers, looking also at their backgrounds, the circumstances leading them to war, and the effect that it had on their lives. Later we look at the effect the war had on the Welsh community in Patagonia.

This book would not have been possible without the help of many people on both sides. In Patagonia I was wholly dependent on others to show me from place to place, to interpret during interviews, to seek out contacts and get hold of information. It would be impossible to acknowledge everyone who helped by name, but among them were Vali James de Irianni,, Luned Gonzalez, Aira Hughes, Benjamin Lewis, Tegai Roberts and Rhona Gough. In Wales, Monica and Gwyn Jones translated the interviews I recorded in Spanish, and I received valuable advice from Tweli Griffiths, Elvey MacDonald and Ceris Gruffudd from the Wales-Argentina Society and the National Library of Wales. My thanks go to the team at Gwasg Carreg Gwalch, especially my editor Angharad Dafis, for their support, patience and attention to detail. My biggest thanks go to everyone, soldiers and civilians, who were so willing to be asked about their experiences, nightmarish for many and which no one, in Wales or Y Wladfa, would ever want to go through again.

Ioan Roberts
October 2003

1. GWLADFAWYR AND KELPERS

It was an unexpected pleasure to meet Tomi Davies of Hyde Park once again. Our first meeting had been in 1990, when the *Hel Straeon* TV crew landed there at short notice to record a conversation with him and his brother Edward. Out of ten brothers only the pair of them remained, two old bachelors on a farm almost as old as Y Wladfa and a chronicle of the community's history. We filmed the two of them working the water wheel they had built themselves with empty paint tins to channel the waters of the Chubut through their farmland. And we recorded Edward playing 'Mochyn Du' and 'Sosban Fach' on the harmonium. The farm had been named after another Welsh community, in Scranton, Pennsylvania. Coming from that Hyde Park, Tomi and Edward's father arrived here at the age of 16 in 1875, ten years after the *Mimosa* landed.

By my next visit to Y Wladfa in 2002, Edward had died and Tomi was living alone in Hyde Park, very frugally so rumour had it. We hadn't intended calling on him, but when our driver parked by the farmyard so that we could have a look at the place, who should pop out of the house but Tomi himself, and he invited us in. He was within a week of his 95th birthday, his stoop pronounced and eyesight fading almost completely. But his memory, mind and speech were as nimble as ever. He talked about how one of the brothers,

Wil, had learned the language of the indigenous people and made friends with them. 'Good people, the Indians,' he said. 'Honest people. An Indian would never lie to you. He would never steal, except to have food. If a mother didn't have enough milk for her baby she would feed it the egg of an ostrich. They had a lot to teach us. Wise people.' Then he added, more in mischief than sadness: 'The Indian language has died, Welsh is dying, and I'm on my way out – might as well just go!'

Although he was never in Wales, Tomi, according to one of his neighbours, is more at home speaking Welsh than Spanish. But that makes him no less of an Argentinian than the people around him. During that chat with the two brothers back in 1990, Gwyn Llewelyn asked them whether they were Welsh or Argentinian. Their answers showed that identity isn't always a matter of black and white:

Edward (definite): Argentinian
Tomi (hesitantly): Yes... sure...
Gwyn: You don't think of yourselves as Welsh?
Edward: No, only that we speak it.
Tomi: Yes, we're Welsh of course.
Edward: Well yes, we are Welsh.
Tomi: But Argentinian isn't it, born in Argentina...

To the east, three hundred miles from the coast of Patagonia, there are people who have no doubt at all concerning who they belong to. Their first pioneers landed about thirty years before the *Mimosa*'s voyage to Patagonia. In the Falkland Islands, as in Unionist parts of Northern Ireland, the Union Jack is more important even than in England. The right to drive on the left was one of the principles being fought over in 1982. The brief visit of the Argentinians that year resulted in the custom of singing 'God Save the Queen' at the end of church services being given up for a while. But the Welsh who settled Y Wladfa had their own words to go with that tune, ending in a rather optimistic prophecy:

> We can go there in peace
> No treachery or sword
> A Welshman on the throne;
> Thanks be to God.

The difference in outlook between the Falklands British and Patagonian Welsh is noted by Max Hastings and Simon Jenkins in their book *The Battle for the Falklands*:

> The descendants of Scots and Welsh settlers in adjacent Patagonia might superficially seem to possess similar characteristics to the Falklanders. Yet even the Welsh of Puerto Madryn are fully fledged Argentinians and proud of it. Their lingua franca is Spanish (or Welsh), not English. The Falklanders, as one of them proudly said, have 'not an ounce of Latin America' in them.

The early settlement in the Falklands was part of British colonial expansion, and the Empire had reason and resources enough to support and defend it. Escaping the grasp of colonialism and English culture was one of the incentives that brought the Welsh to Patagonia. So after getting there and seeing that the Welsh independence dream of some founders was in the event not practical, nothing remained but to make the best of it and adapt in some measure to their new Argentinian homeland.

One reason why Argentina welcomed them was that the space they were occupying might otherwise have beeen colonised by someone else. The most obvious threat in that respect was posed by Britain which, in their view, had stolen the Malvinas some thirty years earlier. And yet, at times of tension, the Argentinian authorities would question the people of Y Wladfa's intentions and see them as potentially part of the colonialism they had in fact fled from, which was now targeting South America. The existence of the Malvinas had therefore an indirect influence on the life of Y Wladfa from the very beginning. Because Patagonians were the islanders' closest neighbours, some economic and social links were inevitably established over the years. It has been said that some early Patagonian Welsh, when times got hard, were tempted to pack their bags and move to the islands. According to Elvey MacDonald, an authority on the history of Y Wladfa, this story has been exaggerated:

> In 1867 a petition was sent to the islands signed by 19 people from Y Wladfa. It was discovered later that most of those listed as signatories were unaware of the petition. There were several children on the list as well. The petition asked the governor of the islands to secure a ship to take them from Y Wladfa, but without saying that they wished to sail to the islands. I would have thought that the intention was to return to Britain. The assumption was, I suspect, that any ship going to or from the islands could call at Y Wladfa to collect the disaffected nineteen. But that did not happen. From this the myth arose that an attempt was made by some to move to the islands.

* * *

Joseph Seth Jones, one of the 150 who voyaged on the

Mimosa to settle Y Wladfa in 1865, left a diary recording the crossing for posterity. A year or two later, when times were hard, he worked his passage to the Falkland Islands. But things were little better there and by 1868 he was back home again in Flintshire. In a letter to *Y Faner* he offered an unbiased assessment of the islands. 'If it is appropriate to compare animals,' he said, 'Pharoah's lean cattle were fatter than the fattest cows in Stanley.'

This was a charitable description compared with the judgment of the Englishman Samuel Johnson. The place, he said, is stormy in the winter and bare in summer: 'an island which not even the southern savages have graced with habitation.' The present inhabitants of the islands, the 'Kelpers', would certainly say that descriptions such as this are grossly unfair to their birthplace. But there are no obvious material gains here to justify the 1982 war, which was described by Jorge Luis Borges as comparable to two bald men fighting over a comb.

The bone of contention is a little older than the Argentinian state, and to do with the colonial ambitions of Spain, Britain and France. The first man documented to have seen the islands was not from any of these countries: Simon de Weert was a Dutch sailor, who passed by in 1600. It seems that the first to set foot on the territory was Captain John Strong, an Englishman who landed there during a storm in 1690 and named the strait between the two main islands Falkland Sound, in honour of the head of the British navy. In 1764 Louis-Antoine de Bougainville sailed there from St Malo in Brittany. He established the first community to remain on the islands, at Port Louis on East Island, and claimed them in the name of France. It was a fisherman from St Malo in Britanny who named them Iles Malouines, after his home port. From this derived the Spanish names Islas

Malvinas, which is therefore a name with a Celtic connection. Shortly afterwards an English mariner arrived to establish Port Egmont on West Falkland, resulting in the first international dispute over sovereignty, between Britain and France.

In 1767 Spain decided to put its finger in the pie. The Spanish believed that under a preceding treaty the islands were part of their South American territory. They paid the French off to make them leave Port Louis, and two years later sent ships and soldiers to expel the English from Port Egmont. After all sorts of threats Britain was allowed to send its citizens back there 'to restore the honour of the king' on condition that they recognized Spain's sovereignty over the islands. Things remained thus until 1774 when the British left again, leaving a plaque behind claiming that they were still the owners.

In 1816 the Argentinian state came into being, declaring its independence from Spain. It claimed sovereignty over all Spanish territory in the region, including the Malvinas. By then Spain's military forces had left the islands to defend possessions on the mainland. Only pirates, criminals and occasional fishermen lived there until 1820, when the new government in Buenos Aires sent a ship and appointed military officials to protect its rights. In 1826 the Argentinians established their first community at Puerto Soledad, with a man named Louis Vernet as Governor.

The 1830s became a turbulent decade for the islands. At that time events took place that were to lead to the war a century and a half later. In 1831 Vernet stopped American ships from whaling in the islands' waters. Encouraged by the British consul in Buenos Aires, the Americans sent the warship *Lexington* in to 'teach the Governor a lesson'. They destroyed a fort in Puerto Soledad then sent Vernet and his officials home, announcing that America had never recognized Argentina's right to be on the islands. In the chaos that followed, Buenos Aires sent another governor to take Vernet's place, and he was murdered by raiders from his own country.

In 1833 Britain saw its chance. The Prime Minister, Palmerston, sent two warships to the islands to raise the union jack and supplant the Argentinians. The only opposition came from a crew of wild gauchos from the mainland, led by one Antonio Rivero. It took six months for the English to get the place under control and in Argentina Rivero is to this day a national hero. But that's when Britain started seriously colonizing the islands, the unlawful work of the bully in the eyes of Argentina, leaving a deep scar on the self-esteem of the young nation.

Through the years Argentina has never stopped insisting that it has the legal and historical right to the islands. There has been much diplomatic deliberation on the subject , with Britain from time to time recognizing privately that the Argentinian claims have some foundation. After the British empire declined, remote territories on the other side of the world began to be seen as expensive and unnecessary. Two years before the war, one of Mrs Thatcher's most trusted ministers, Nicholas Ridley, introduced a lease back plan to the House of Commons, which would have transferred sovereignty of the islands to Argentina. The islanders were sensing the possibility of betrayal by the mother country.

Then Leopoldo Galtieri, to the world's amazement, decided to take the islands back by force. He was the third military dictator to have run Argentina since the army coup in 1976 leading to the 'dirty war' which saw thousands of activists on the left victimized and murdered. Galtieri's main aim in sending troops to the Malvinas was to divert attention from his country's economic problems. It worked at first, with crowds once against him celebrating, within days, on the streets of Buenos Aires. Galtieri had anticipated support from his anti-communist ally Ronald Reagan. But this never materialized. Galtieri also thought that Britain, who had just announced the withdrawal of their single warship, the *Endurance*, from the area, would not care enough about the islands to go to war on their behalf. His greatest mistake was to take action during the reign of Margaret Thatcher, a leader as prepared as he was to use bloodshed for her own ends.

The result was an old fashioned colonial war that looked stupid to the rest of the world. Around 1800 people lived on the islands at the time, and about a thousand, between the two sides, were killed in the war to free them. Since then the Falklands are thriving, the population increasing, and British tax payers hand over £70 million a year to defend then. The islanders no longer have to worry that they will be betrayed by the mother country, and much of the thanks for that must go to Leopoldo Galtieri.

And Welsh Patagonia? For the first time in its history, the use of the Welsh language among young people there is on the rise, the result of a plan to promote its use, which started with the Welsh Office and has since extended to the Welsh Assembly. This involves paying salaries and expenses for three Welsh teachers to go to Y Wladfa each year, also supporting a number of local teachers in learning Welsh, and contributing to the expenses of four students from Y Wladfa who come to study annually at the University of Wales in Lampeter. The cost of all this is £35,000 per year, one two thousandth of the cost of defending the Falklands. The teachers' programme started following a commitment made by a minister from the Welsh Office during a visit to Y Wladfa at the beginning of the 1990s. His name was Rod

Richards. If the Kelpers have reason to thank Galtieri for protecting their Britishness, the people of Y Wladfa, beneficiaries of this boost to their Welshness, owe a debt too to the political party of Margaret Thatcher.

2. CHRONICLE 1982

March 19
Scrap dealers and a handful of soldiers from Argentina land on the island of South Georgia and raise the Argentinian flag.

April 2
Thousands of Argentinian soldiers land on the Malvinas. A group of British Marines engages them.

April 3
Argentinian soldiers take South Georgia and the South Sandwich Islands.
The United Nations calls on Argentina to leave the islands.

April 5-8
Eight thousand British Task Force troops leave Portsmouth and Southampton on their way to the South Atlantic.

April 8
US Secretary of State, Alexander Haig, arrives in London attempting to start up negotiations.

April 17
Haig holds talks with the Buenos Aires government.

April 25
British Commandos retake South Georgia.

April 30
Ronald Reagan announces that the United States is supporting Britain and initiates sanctions against Argentina.

May 2
The President of Peru proposes a peace plan to Galtieri. The Argentinian President accepts it with some amendments. The most controversial occurence of the war takes place as the submarine *HMS Conqueror* sinks the *General Belgrano* outside the exclusion zone imposed by Britain. Close to 400 are killed. The junta rejects the Peruvian plan.

May 4
The Argentinian Air Force sinks *HMS Sheffield*.

May 7
The United Nations starts peace talks.

May 14
The SAS launches a night attack on one of the smaller islands, Pebble Island, destroying a number of Argentinian warplanes.

May 18
Britain rejects UN Secretary General Perez de Quellar's peace plan.

May 21
British forces land near Port San Carlos on East Falkland and establish their HQ there.

HMS Ardent is sunk by the Argentinian Air Force.

May 25
HMS Coventry and the *Atlantic Conveyor* are hit.

May 28
2 Para Regiment wins the battles of Darwin and Goose Green. Around 200 Argentinians and 17 British soldiers are killed.

May 31
British soldiers capture Mount Kent and surround Port Stanley.

June 4
At the UN Security Council Britain vetoes the peace plan put forward by Panama and Spain.

June 6
A meeting of world leaders at Versailles backs Britain's position on the islands.

June 8
The Argentinian Air Force attacks the *Sir Galahad* and *Sir Tristram* at Bluff Cove. 31 members of the Welsh Guards are among the 50 killed.

June 12
Britain wins the battles of Mount Longdon, Two Sisters and Mount Harriet.
HMS Glamorgan is hit by an Exocet missile.

June 14

Commander of the Argentinian Forces, General Menendez, signs the Peace Agreement.

June 17

Galtieri is forced to resign after speaking out against this plan, and the reign of the military junta is brought to an end.

June 20

Britain formally declares that the war is over.

Late June

More than 17,000 Argentinian prisoners of war are taken home.

THE BATTLEFIELD

3. BRONWEN WILLIAMS,
PORT STANLEY

If you had asked a Welsh person before 1982 where the Falklands were, the most likely answer would have been 'somewhere in Scotland'. Many of the troops sent there assumed something similar initially before suddenly finding out, in the words of one Welsh Guardsman, that 'it was a hell of a long way further than that'. It was to Scotland though, not to the South Atlantic or South America, that I had to travel to hear an account of the Argentinian landing in Port Stanley, as seen through the eyes of a resident there at the time. It was in the pretty and historic town of Haddington, fifteen miles south west of Edinburgh, that I met Bronwen Douse, or Bronwen Williams as she was at the time of the war.

Bronwen was the Welsh nurse who met an Argentinian soldier of Welsh heritage in church in Port Stanley. The encounter has been over-romanticized, but the story served to illustrate the tragedy of the Falklands/Malvinas conflict, and indeed, of wars in general. I had met the soldier, Milton Rhys, in Y Wladfa in 1990. At about the same time I learned that the nurse, Bronwen, had family in the village of Cegidfa, on the outskirts of Welshpool, and that she was working as a nurse in Shrewsbury. But where was she by this time? Living in a small country sometimes has its advantages.

Idwal Davies, formerly a reporter for the *County Times*, knows almost everyone in Montgomeryshire, but surprisingly he didn't know Bronwen. He gave me though the number of their ex-editor, George McHardy, who lived in Cegidfa. No, he didn't know Bronwen either, but he would ask his wife, who knew everyone in the village. She phoned back within five minutes, and I left for Cegidfa to knock at the door of Mrs Betty Williams, a lady originally from Dyfnaint. She confirmed that she was Bronwen's mother, and that Bronwen was now married with two daughters of her own and living in Scotland.

When I reached the house in Haddington months later it was by then touch and go; another month and I would have had to travel far further. Bronwen and her family were about to up sticks and go to live once again in the Falklands. But busy as she was with the packing, Bronwen found time to talk me through her background, and to recall that turbulent year of 1982.

My grandfather on my father's side was the Reverend Hywel Williams. Elen Jones was my grandmother's maiden name, and both came originally from Blaenau Ffestiniog. At one time my grandfather was a minister in Oswestry. where my father, Ieuan Meirion Williams, was born. Years later he and my mother retired to Cegidfa, in the same area, after he had worked in London as a dentist for most of his life.

I did my general nursing training in London, and trained as a midwife in Shrewsbury. For two and a half years I worked among the Labrador Eskimos, then I came home to visit the family and stayed longer than I had intended after my father had a stroke. Then I went to the Falklands in October 1980. All I wanted was a rural life, and to live in a small community with the opportunity to give continuous care to the same people, instead of being a nurse who dealt with strangers all the time. They knew you, and you knew them. You knew what treatment they'd received from you in the past, and you knew of their way of life, and you hoped that the care you gave them meant something personal to them and their lives.

I knew nothing before going there about the argument over who owned the islands. So the events of April 1982 came as a bit of a shock! We had been warned over the radio by the Governor, Rex Hunt, at about eight o'clock the previous evening that the Argentine Navy was at sea and heading in our direction. And of course we were aware of the strange events with the scrap metal dealers in South Georgia earlier, which had left us all nervous and wondering what on earth was going on. The warning didn't give us much time to prepare in the hospital for what was ahead of us, but we made arrangements to move the older patients to the safest part of the building if it became necessary.

I was at work that morning, and at about seven or eight, we heard the sound of gunfire. We listened the whole time to the local radio for news of what was happening. Then someone telephoned to say that the first casualties were on their way to us. They were Argentinians who had been shot outside Government House. We were almost next door to that building, so they didn't have far to come to get to the hospital.

It was a very strange feeling. Here we were giving exactly the same medical and nursing care to these people as we would to our own. We were trying to save the lives of people who had been shot as they tried to attack us, which didn't make much sense.

I remember there were three of them who had been shot by the Royal Marines on the periphery of Government House. They wore bullet-proof vests but the bullets had somehow got though them. The other thing I remember clearly was that the medical crew who came into the hospital with the Argentinians were still carrying their weapons, as if they expected that we had guns as well in the hospital, which was very strange. We persuaded them to leave their weapons at the door. Then we worked together as a team to the best of our ability, in spite of the language difficulties, to try to save these people. But once it was obvious that no more could be done, they cleared up after them and went, shaking our hands and saying 'Cheerio' as if they had just called to clean the windows, which again was strange. It was as if all normal circumstances had been temporarily suspended. But I was proud that we had all managed to work together effectively in the medical setting and do our best for the casualties. There was no suggestion at all that we had failed to do our best only because they had invaded us. Two of the casualties died but, if I remember rightly, the Argentinians took the third away somewhere. We never discovered what happened to him.

Later that day, when we were feeling brave enough to look through the window after taking shelter in the most secure part of the building, it was a frightening sight seeing the tanks grinding up the narrow village lanes, their gun turrets on top turning as if they expected us to fire on them, while we didn't have a single gun between us. It looked a complete farce, with the width of the tank filling the whole road, as if you lived in a quiet British village, looked out of the window and suddenly saw a tank coming towards you. We were offering them no threat at all, and the whole thing was terrifying. They weren't shooting at us of course, just wary of what they might encounter.

The Royal Marines were our only defence, and normally we only had 40 of them, on secondment from Britain. But at this point some of them had returned home and a further 40 had arrived to take their place, so when the invasion came there were about 60 Marines on the islands, the largest number during that year.

After the first day we didn't treat many battle wounds in the hospital. It was a long, narrow building with one area, where I worked, reserved for serious cases. The other end was more like a care home. The Argentinians decided that they would take over that end of the hospital. They put up a curtain dividing the building into two halves, so we didn't see many of their wounded.

I remember how I would wake up some fine mornings, with everything so peaceful and the sun shining on a calm sea. I would look out of the window and wonder, 'How is it possible to be so peaceful here in the middle of a war?' We became quite organised and disciplined in the way we managed our lives. Once they announced a curfew, which meant that we couldn't be out on the streets after half-past four in the afternoon. We knew that we had to finish our shopping before that time, and anything else that involved being outdoors. Because I worked in the hospital, I often had to rely on others to shop for me. But we worked well together as a community and I remember thinking that this sounded similar to that spirit during the second world war, as my parents described it. They remembered the camaraderie, with everyone helping each other. We certainly experienced the same feeling.

We were lucky in one thing,- it was never a problem

getting enough to eat. In the Falklands the supply ship only arrived two or three times a year, so we were well used to keeping a good stock of provisions. This was also true of the shops. They always had plenty in to keep them going. We were used to the supply ships being delayed by bad weather so we made sure we had plenty in reserve.

So for us there were no shortages, but supplies were clearly a problem for the Argentinians. We could see that they weren't being properly fed and they often went around the houses with their guns, wanting to get food. It was pitiful to be honest, and we would often feel sorry for them. But this was hard for us too, because we didn't want to get caught up in the politics of the whole thing. If you gave them any food, another twenty would then arrive minutes later. Some of them were very courteous but others could be confrontational, and you were never quite sure what to expect. In the hospital we would sometimes get Argentinian soldiers turning up with their guns demanding to see some paperwork or other or wanting to carry out a search. But then some of the officers who spoke English would call by, full of apologies for the intrusion earlier. As soon as those had gone another wild lot would turn up. We never knew where we stood with them.

It was very difficult for us to keep in touch with everyone on the islands and make sure they were alright. I remember the family doctor who was there at the time saying how she made contact by radio in the mornings to check if everyone was well in all the different communities. At one time there had been some trouble on Pebble Island, one of the smallest, and the community there weren't making contact by radio with Port Stanley. So the doctor had no way of knowing how everyone was.

But she did know that all the people of the island were together in one large house, and that smoke rising from the chimney could be seen from one of the neighbouring islands. So the doctor could call up the other island on the radio and ask 'How's the bobble hat?' This refered to a man from a Welsh background, Griff Evans, the community leader on Pebble Island, who always wore a knitted bobble hat. If the answer was that there was smoke coming out of the chimney, she knew that everything was fine or, at least, that they could still keep a fire going in the Raeburn. So there were many ways of checking up on people even though, at times, the Argentinians would prevent any communication they had doubts about or that they felt could lead to contact with Britain.

Once, during the war, someone in Wales told my mother that they had heard about me on the Welsh radio news. As they understood it, I had been taken from the island, and they were asking whether she knew anything about that. My mother doesn't understand Welsh, and she hadn't heard the story herself. But apparently it was reported that the Argentinians had evicted me from the hospital, along with the rest of the staff. That hadn't happened either, but it was a possibility at one time. Somewhere in the course of the news being translated from Welsh, one word had been misunderstood and the story altered so she thought that I had left the islands. But she did get to know the truth because we had a network of people who were in contact, exchanging news and boosting each other's morale. A family from Dyfnaint was part of that, communicating by amateur radio with Saunders Island which was, in turn, in contact with Pebble Island. This way I managed to get a message to my mother telling her that I was fine and in Port Stanley. This went from me to Pebble, from there to Saunders, and via amateur radio to Dyfnaint where they were able to get on the phone to my mother telling her not to worry, that Bronwen was fine. This was a great relief to her. A lot of that kind of networking was going on, people finding all sorts of ways to pass on information.

It was at church in Stanley that I met Milton Rhys. He had come to the service looking distinctly unhappy and it was obvious that the whole thing was a bit of a strain for him. He was sitting at the back and I was in my usual place near the front. I remember thinking as we slowly left at the end that someone would surely say something to him. I didn't believe that a congregation on their way out of a religious service would ignore someone sad and alone without saying something to him. I remembered the story of the Good Samaritan and I didn't want to pass by him on the other side. It was obvious that he had come to church to worship, and not just to see what was happening. So, as we were all still slowly walking out, busy with chat and reassuring each other, I decided that if no one else had approached him by the time I drew near his seat I would say something to him so that he wouldn't feel ignored. At the same time I was churning inside and thinking, 'Why am I doing this? Do I think I'm cleverer and more Christian than these other people? No, I promise I'll do this if no one else does.' As I drew alongside Milton's seat I was aware that everyone else would be looking at me. But I went over to him, and I said something brief, something like 'Bless you, I'm sorry you've been caught up in a situation like this.' And I headed straight for the door before people could think I was collaborating with the enemy or anything like that.

I had a message to give to the Minister, the Reverend

Harry Bagnell, and I stood by the door until he was free to speak. While I was still waiting for him I noticed that he had gone to chat to Milton, and then he called me. 'Come here, Bronwen',' he said. 'Come and speak to this boy here. It's possible you may be related - he comes from Wales!'

It was a really strange feeling. Such a coincidence. And I couldn't help thinking that perhaps this kind of connection between people could help heal the wounds after a war, and promote international peace. I felt we were in a situation, alone and in the middle of that community, which involved greater and wider obligations than those apparent at first glance.

Milton came to church many times after that. Though I was convinced that he was there for the service, others in the congregation weren't so sure. Some thought he was there to watch us and listen to what the minister spoke about and that sort of thing. I remember arriving late one Sunday and sitting at the back. Milton arrived later and there was nowhere for him to sit. He looked at me politely, as if to ask whether there was room in the pew, and of course I invited him to sit. He had no hymn book, and didn't know where they were kept so I shared mine with him. That, somehow, felt significant, willingly sharing a hymn book during a war with someone from the other side.

After realising that we were both from Welsh communities, it was obvious to us that we had much in common. At the end of one service he showed me a cutting from his local newspaper in Patagonia, explaining that his mother had included it in a letter. It was a report of an eisteddfod he had taken part in before leaving Argentina. A strange feeling arose from this too. It could easily have been me receiving a letter from my mother with a cutting from the *County Times* about an eisteddfod in Montgomeryshire. All this made you think about the waste of war. All that gets proved is who can hit the hardest, not who is right or wrong.

At the end of the war there was heavy fighting in Stanley and Government House where Milton had spent most of his time was bombed. He phoned us at the hospital later to let us know he was fine. The British soldiers had treated him well, he said. He had been slightly injured, but nothing serious.

He was very courteous. We exchanged addresses in case the opportunity arose to meet up after all this was over. And he wrote to my mother to say how glad he was to have met me. Looking back, this had been a turning point in my own life. Previously I had met hardly any Argentinians to speak with, other than a few doctors. And after realising that there were people on their side who wanted no part in the trouble, and had no personal ill-feeling towards us, I saw the whole thing in a new light. This left me with strong views about war and peace, and how we should foster understanding to stop matters from heading towards war.

Out of nearly a thousand people who lost their lives during the war, all but three were members of the armed forces on either side. One of the three exceptions was a close friend of Bronwen's. She too was Welsh, from Llandrindod.

Susan Whitley was her name, the same age as me and married to the islands' vet. She was killed during the shelling. I had been speaking to her earlier that afternoon. It could so easily have been me, and that made me think about how precarious the situation was for all of us.

I learned an awful lot during that time. It helped me confirm my true priorities in life, and realise what is important. I don't think I'm in a position to say whether the war was of any value, because it's impossible to weigh and measure precisely what was in the balance on either side. But I certainly felt that the price paid in suffering, death and the wounds inflicted on the soldiers was a very high price to pay for our freedom. Obviously I wish that the whole thing had been avoided. And this left me with a burden to be carried regarding what I should do with the rest of my life, given that my freedom had cost so much. There comes a point where you have to carry on and do your best. But I'm sure some of the lessons will stay with me for the rest of my life.

The war was not all bad for Bronwen. That was when she met her husband, Andrew Douse, who was working on the islands as an ecologist.

He was the 'Goose Officer' on the islands! He studied wild geese there, birds that were a bit of a pest for farmers. As soon as they had sown new grass seed for the sheep pasture, these geese would arrive and start feasting - and Andrew was looking for ways to deal with the problem.

The house where he lived had been hit during the fighting and he had no electricity or water. He had also volunteered to work in the hospital; they were looking for young men with no family ties to come and help out. He had nowhere to live and I told him he could stay with me, on condition that he behaved himself - and he did! We became close friends, and in 1983 we came back home to Wales, to marry in Cegidfa.

In April 2003 Bronwen, Andrew and their younger daughter Frances moved back to the Falklands. Their elder daughter Elinor stayed behind to finish her course at Newcastle University. Andrew had been offered a two year research contract studying ways of preserving the islands' biodiversity. Bronwen went back to work in the same Port Stanley hospital where she experienced the challenging events of 1982.

Returning to the South Atlantic she hoped to meet Milton Rhys again, possibly in Patagonia or even at the church in Port Stanley, but without war raging in the background.

4. MILTON RHYS, TRELEW

Milton Rhys and I are sitting in the garden of one of the Welsh tea houses in Gaiman, discussing a topic I know nothing about, the Welsh instrumental music known as cerdd dant. As it does from morning to night in *Tŷ Gwyn*, the voice of Dafydd Iwan drifts out through the window singing 'Paentio'r Byd yn Wyrdd'. Gaiman is Y Wladfa's most Welsh village, and this is reflected in *Tŷ Gwyn*, where I was staying. Milton speaks only a little Welsh, but there's one feat he can perform for me, which is singing in the language.

He asked what the difference is between cerdd dant and canu pennillion. I answered, as if I understand all these things, that there's none as far as I know, no difference except for the name. Milton was familiar with one of the terms but not the other, and that caused a confusion which resulted in his daughter losing a prize at an eisteddfod for breaking the rules of the competition. Welsh visitors to Patagonia are met with some wonderfully familiar experiences as well as the foreign ones.

But here we were discussing darker matters than a Welsh musical conundrum. Milton, who looks a little too young to go to war even today, spent the Malvinas conflict in Government House in Port Stanley - or Puerto Argentino as Argentinians call the only town on the islands. Government House was caught in the middle of the fighting, and one of

Milton's tasks was to wash the socks of the head of the Argentinian forces, General Mario Menendez. Because of Milton, through no fault of his own, the myth arose that this army was full of soldiers who spoke the Welsh language.

Milton's Welsh roots go back four generations, to the early days of Y Wladfa. One of his ancestors was the Reverend William Casnodyn Rhys, a poet and minister from the Port Talbot area, who established the first Welsh Baptist chapel in Patagonia. The fate of that building, ironic given its Baptist denomination, was to be destroyed by water in a flood. The Chair for best poet, won by Casnodyn in Eisteddfod y Wladfa, in 1881, is on display at Gaiman's Museum, and the story of the chairing is part of Rhys family lore. Casnodyn himself was master of ceremonies on that occasion and, after calling twice, without response, for the winning poet, under his pseudonym 'Meidrol', to stand up and be recognized, he pretended to lose his balance before sitting down in the chair himself.

William Casnodyn Rhys was head of the Chubut Co-operative Society and secretary to Gaiman Town Council, before returning to Wales with his family after retiring. But one of his sons, David Ifor Rhys, returned to Y Wladfa with his wife to farm in the Treorcki area. One of their sons, Leslie, founded an English language teacher's training college in Trelew. Milton Rhys is his son.

Milton spent five years of his childhood in the United States, where he became fluent in English. He and his sister run the college their father established, by now a university. His greatest interest is in music, and he leads a number of choirs. He lives in Trelew with his wife Alexandra and their children Astrid, Gretel and Dennis, all three of them pupils at Ysgol Dewi Sant in Trelew and learning to speak Welsh.

At the beginning of the 1980s Milton had been at

university for a year before having to leave to do his military service. After that his life was shattered by the war in the Malvinas. He says that it took twenty years for him to be able to speak openly about his experiences.

At that time every Argentinian boy, when he turned 18, had to do his military training for between one and three years. In my case it was to last a year and I was allowed to do my service in Trelew, where I lived. I was being trained to do radio work, learning the military applications, how to use code and so on. I had my twentieth birthday in January 1982 and was looking forward to my release the following month. But when March came I was still there. Three of us were working together in the unit, we understood our work and we never had any problem with our superiors.

But that changed for me a week before the end of my military service. I had an argument with the Colonel in charge of the army in the area. He was drunk that night and things turned bad. So I ended my service in the dungeon at a military prison. I was allowed out on the evening on April 2nd, thinking 'Well thank goodness, here I am free.' In prison I had heard nothing about what was happening outside. But when I got home my father said: 'It's a good thing you're out of military service – Argentina has reoccupied the Malvinas! Thank goodness you're home.'

But the next day, at nine in the morning, who called at the house but the Colonel who had just put me in prison. 'You're going to the Malvinas,' he said. 'To do what?' I asked. 'You understand radio and you can speak English. You can go there as a translator.'

So off I went that day, alone and wearing my own

clothes, to Comodoro Rivadavia where everything was being organised. By April 5th I was on a Hercules flying to the islands. When I reached Puerto Argentino I was still in my own clothes. I asked where Government House was and who was responsible for the soldiers. Two days later I introduced myself to the chief, General Daher. He was responsible, at the beginning, for the troops in Puerto Argentino. I had never met a General before. I was still in my own clothes but carrying my uniform in a bag – they had said that I would have to wear it. 'You can stay with me,' said Daher, 'and since you're Welsh you can make me a cup of tea.' I made a cup, and he poured a drop of whisky in before drinking it. He was drunk half the time, very like Galtieri in that respect.

I did nothing for a day or two then Daher said I should translate some messages in English that they had recorded. Then the authorities moved Daher somewhere else and Menendez came to us in his place. Daher introduced me to him. 'This boy has a Welsh and English heritage,' he said, 'and he can be a help to you in all this.'

I had been sleeping at night, along with the other soldiers, in a hole we had dug in the ground, which kept filling up with water all the time. But Menendez let me sleep in Government House, which had been home to Rex Hunt and his family. Sleeping on the floor, true, but at least it was dry.

Menendez was a bit more civilized than Daher. I wouldn't say we were friends but I did get to know him fairly well. I took his coffee to him in the morning and would even wash his socks. He asked me once to make maté (the leaf drink popular in Argentina) for him. I didn't drink maté myself at that time, and I made the mistake of boiling the water first, which ruins it. When I gave the maté to Menendez he spat it out. 'Rhys, are you a Welshman?' 'Si, mon General.' 'Make me a cup of tea!'

He was a gentleman, and considerate. He had concern for his soldiers, and for the injured on both sides. You would have to condemn his role in the 'dirty war' some years earlier though – I don't think anyone has looked properly into those events.

My main work was translating and typing for Menendez. There was often a need for translation when there were things to discuss with the people of the islands. Afterwards when the fighting started they would always take a translator with them to the battle front. The idea was that we would need an interpreter after we took British soldiers prisoner. Our spirits were so high then that no one even considered we might lose the war. I did translate two or three times in that situation, but most of the work was to do with day to day problems like getting petrol for the vehicles or peat for the stoves, or talking to a plumber when there was a problem with water.

I was still working with radio transmissions and would type up a single-page news sheet for our soldiers. Another time I was peeling potatoes and helping in the kitchen, and having to be on guard at night three or four times each week. We were all getting very little sleep and the British forces were good at psychological warfare. They would bombard us for ten minutes until everyone was awake, leave us alone for two hours to get back to sleep, then start it up again. By the end nobody on the islands was sleeping at all, not the soldiers on either side or the islanders. It must have been a terrible thing for the islanders, so far from their usual simple and quiet life, with this dreadful war suddenly on their doorstep.

No one would believe how little preparation we had

as soldiers for being at war. I'm not talking about the professional soldiers, but the majority of us who were conscripts. I learnt more in my time as a boy scout than during all the military training. I hadn't had my hands on a gun, except for hunting foxes and rabbits on the farm in Gaiman. I had certainly never pointed a firearm at a human being. So when they gave me a gun on the island I had no idea what to do with it. 'You've been trained,' they said. 'Only trained to use radio equipment,' I replied. So they took me to a place at the edge of the town and showed me how to open the gun, clean, load and shoot it.

It was better for me than for a lot of the others there though. Some of the young boys had been brought up on the pampas, had never seen the sea or traveled on a boat or a plane, had little education – some couldn't even write their names. And suddenly here they were in the middle of a war. Against whom? Britishers? Europeans? Fighting for what? The Malvinas? Where's that? They had never heard of the place before, and here they were, for more than 70 days, sleeping with their heads in the mud. And all this because Galtieri and his men wanted to hold on to their power for a little while longer.

I was getting on very well with the people of the island. I became friends with one man called Mr Don. He was the Governor Rex Hunt's chauffeur, a generous and intelligent enough man in his own slow way. I think he belonged to the fifth generation of his family on the island, and he had children and grandchildren. That's seven generations in all. I'm the fourth generation in Argentina. Yes, I got on well with the islanders but not so well, on the whole, with people from Britain who were only there to work for a year or two.

The *Liverpool Daily Post* for 24th October 1989 included the headline 'When the Argies spoke Welsh'. In the article below it, their reporter, Ivor Wynne Jones, described his conversation with Don Bonner, Governor Rex Hunt's chauffeur – 'Mr Don'. Don Bonner said he had learnt to sing 'Land of my Fathers' from a Welsh head teacher when he was a schoolboy in Port Stanley. During World War 2 he had also spent some of his military training at *HMS Glendower*, which later became the Butlin's Holiday Camp in Pwlleli.

'I know when I'm hearing Welsh and I was very surprised to hear it at Government House,' he told the reporter. The only 'Welsh speaker' he named was the 'junior NCO called Milton-Rees' (sic). But he stated that there were 'several Welsh-speaking guards' among the Argentinians in Government House. He had also heard, he claimed, a number of young Argentinians speaking Welsh after coming ashore from the hospital ship.

He had good things to say about Milton. 'Milton-Rees was a likeable young man and we used to have long discussions about the Argentinian claims to the Falkland Islands,' he said. Milton's final words as he was being taken by ship back to Argentina as a prisoner were: 'I'm Argentinian and I always will be.'

From chatting with Milton today, it's clear that Mr Don's ear wasn't sufficiently attuned to the differences between Spanish and Welsh, the language of his old headmaster and the people of Pwlleli. Throughout the war Milton came across no soldiers, on either side, who spoke Welsh. His only connection to Wales was meeting Bronwen at the church. He met her there more than once and he can't remember which was the first time. But it is interesting comparing their respective recollections after more than twenty years.

I went to the Anglican church in Puerto Argentino to worship and of course they were very frightened when they saw an Argentinian soldier in uniform walk in. I looked like Rambo, carrying weapons and everything. I left my arms on a bench in the back row to avoid making them nervous.

The service was in English, and they didn't know whether I could speak the language or not. I remember walking down the aisle looking for somewhere to sit, and this young girl and an older woman beside here moved over to make room for me. One was the minister's wife, the other was Bronwen, and we shared a hymn book. Because I read music I was singing tenor within seconds. Bronwen was singing alto, the minister's wife sang the melody, and people were starting to look after realizing that they had a new voice in the congregation. I have never been more aware of how important music is in religious services, and in my own life. I don't remember if it was that time, but Bronwen and I talked and since she was Bronwen Williams and my name is Rhys it didn't take long for us to realise that we were both of Welsh heritage. Meeting Bronwen made me realise the stupidity of the situation we were in being at war.

I had to go to the hospital every now and then to translate and help resolve problems that would arise, and people from the hospital would come to see us in Government House to discuss things like using the football field that was behind the building and next to the hospital.

An unfortunate problem came up when we shot one of the hospital's best cows by accident. The cattle would come to graze on the football field. In the middle of one very dark night we heard a noise close to the house. Two or three strange things had happened over previous days, for example, the cook had asked me to go outside to get vegetables from the garden and when I opened the door what did I see but a grenade. It wasn't an Argentinian one so it must have been British, and I ran to the house to tell the military police. We were pretty sure that British commandos had surrounded the house, and even though we couldn't be certain of that people were nervous and on tenterhooks all the time. So when we heard the noise that night someone shouted 'Halt' in Spanish expecting to hear the password, which was changed each day. But there was no answer so one of the military police shot in the direction of the sound. We had to wait till morning to see what had happened, and it was then that we realised we had shot a cow. I remember General Menendez having a fierce argument with one of the men from the hospital – that was their best milking cow!

A common complaint from Argentinian people since the war is that the truth was kept hidden from them during the fighting. According to Milton even the military leaders themselves were kept in the dark.

Because I was so close to General Menendez you would have thought that I knew pretty well what was going on around us. There's one story especially which shows that wasn't so. Late one night when I was on watch a man came to Government House, knocked hard on the door and asked me where General Menendez was. I asked him to tell me who he was and give me his message - letting him know the General was asleep. He was a senior officer in the Argentinian Air Force and he wanted me to wake Menendez because he had very important news. I did so and this man promptly told him that we had sunk the ship the *Canberra*. He was describing how our plane had fired an Exocet from such and such a distance, and so on.

But when the war was over a British soldier told us that we were going to be taken back home by sea to the mainland. The name of the ship, he said, was the *Canberra*. I was laughing to myself and thinking 'Poor chap, nobody told him that the *Canberra* has been sunk.' When they took us out to the ship, the largest I'd ever been on, I saw the name *Canberra* clearly on her side. And I was still thinking that they'd put that name on a different ship to fool people. But after boarding and seeing the name everywhere I realized that it was us who had been misled. Even Menendez, head of our army, was tricked into thinking that the *Canberra* had been sunk.

Such things were happening nearly every day during the war. I think it was on Radio Montevideo from Uruguay that I heard the *Belgrano* had been sunk. Menendez would ask me to listen to radio stations from different countries to learn what was really happening. It sounds incredible but it's true – the leaders were keeping things hidden even from General Menendez! So when we heard from one of those stations that such and such had happened we would think 'This can't be true.' But usually it was true. It was us getting the false information. Only a drunk – Galtieri especially, but he wasn't the only one – would think of keeping knowledge from his chief military people during wartime.

In the last days before the truce we could see the British soldiers getting closer to the town and the aerial bombardment was getting heavier. I had to go towards the front line that week, but there was no way of making much progress because of the bombing. We had to turn back, seeing our own soldiers walking behind us - many of them injured, the courage and hope drained out of them. It was as if they were in a dream, following a line because that happened to be moving in some direction, walking because they had to walk - after all the days of hunger, cold and sleeplessness, with the deafening explosions of bombs and shells around them.

In the end three mortar bombs fell near Government House, two in front and one behind. When the first landed we were given the order 'Everyone to his station,' and I went to my radio. When the second fell Menendez was talking to Galtieri on the radio telephone. Ten thousand of us can thank Menendez, and that conversation, for our being alive today. 'This is impossible, General,' said Menendez. 'We have no big guns, no strategy, no air support, nothing to throw at them except stones. This isn't war, it's a massacre'. And Galtieri answering, sounding completely drunk, 'Get out of your holes and fight, cowards!' 'If we do that,' said Menendez, 'we will all be corpses. This is not cowardice, we have no way at all to fight and I'm going to surrender.' 'No you will not...' At that moment another bomb landed in the back yard and shattered the radio room. Part of the wall was stone and the rest was wood. The wooden part was blown to bits. And there we were, Menendez and everybody, crouching for shelter by the stone wall. That wall saved our lives. Then I heard the words 'Get out of the house!' I ran out towards the hole in the ground where I'd been based at the start of the war. I had almost reached it when the third bomb fell in front of the house and close to where I was running. We were in line, two or three men in front of me and four or five behind. At least two of those behind me were killed in the blast and I could feel a piece of metal in my back. What saved me was that it had passed through the thick leather strap holding the heavy gun I was carrying. The strap broke and the gun was thrown, along with me, onto the ground. The piece of metal was in my back but the others said the injury wasn't serious and that I should keep on running.

And run I did, towards the centre of Puerto Argentino, thinking they wouldn't bomb there because there were so many islanders around. I could have been wrong as I heard later that they had plans to bomb the centre of the town too if necessary. I went along the sea shore rather than across the open ground, hoping that a bomb would do less damage if it landed on sand or in the sea. I kept on running until I reached the town centre safely.

Menendez and his team had reached there already and made contact with the British through a channel that had been set up by their chief officer, General Jeremy Moore. Before too long – I don't remember if it was minutes or hours – the bombing quietened down and peace came once again to Puerto Argentino.

Soon afterwards I went back to my old workplace in Government House to see if any of my things were still there. It was a shock to see that five or six British soldiers had arrived before me and were going through the place looking for documents, maps and so on. They were armed, as was I – I didn't have the big gun but I did have a revolver, and I'm afraid that my instinctive response was to start taking that out. They looked at me and asked 'What's up with you? Are you stupid?' I saw no one pointing a gun at me but if I had shot it's clear I would have been a dead man. 'Excuse me,' I said sheepishly, and I put the gun away. Then they carried on with their work.

I went to look for my stuff and saw that the radio

equipment was in bits because of the bomb blast. After an hour or two nobody from my office had arrived and I walked once again to the centre of town, where the Argentinian soldiers were gathering.

They treated us well. Mr Don the chauffeur had said to me: 'Inside every British officer you will find a British gentleman.' In my experience that was true on the whole. The exception was one young boy - he was younger than me and youth can trigger all kinds of problems. We almost got into a fight. But apart from that we were treated like professional soldiers, and Don was absolutely right.

After two or three days they told us that we were going by ship back to the mainland. That's when I had the shock of realising that the Canberra hadn't been sunk. There were thousands of us packed in tight on the ship. They fed us and I had a bath for the first time in three months, but like everyone else I had no clean clothes to change into.

They told us that the ship had to be moving before the fresh water system would work properly, so we sailed. Each of us had a compass in his watch and we worked out that we were sailing around the Malvinas, possibly twice. Then we started to sail north. The sailors guarding us had no more idea of where we were going than we did. They thought we were on the way to Uruguay or Brazil.

I was one of two or three hundred sitting on the floor of what had been a ballroom or some such – there was still a piano in there. There wasn't enough room for us to lie down. Two of us spoke English, a boy from La Plata in Buenos Aires province and myself. So we translated when anyone needed anything. This was often, as many of our soldiers were wounded.

I think we were sailing for about three days. Then one morning the officer responsible for us tapped my shoulder and said 'Come outside!' This was an order and I was thinking 'What have I done? What trouble am I in now?' After going out we saw land on the horizon. Before that we had seen nothing because the windows were covered. 'Where is that over there?' asked a British soldier. 'Patagonia or Uruguay?' 'Patagonia' I replied. It wasn't Buenos Aires and it wasn't Uruguay. I wasn't familiar with Brazil but that was Patagonia for sure. I recognized the cliffs though I wasn't sure yet which part of Patagonia – Rio Gallegos perhaps, or Puerto Madryn.

We chatted on for a couple of hours and it was strange, on our way from a war, that the officer had so much interest in Patagonia. What sort of place was Rio Gallegos? What was life like in Puerto Madryn?

As we were talking like this the landscape was becoming clearer and I said 'This is Puerto Madryn for sure. I can see the gulf. That is part of Penninsula Valdes, and Punto Nintas is over there. It must be that we're sailing for Puerto Madryn.' You couldn't mistake this landscape for anywhere else. One minute you saw land, then it wasn't there. We were seeing exactly the view that the first Welsh saw all those years ago, under such different circumstances. And we landed in Puerto Madryn, about three miles from the spot where the *Mimosa* landed in 1865.

Twenty years after the war Milton spoke about his experiences on Tweli Griffiths's TV show on S4C. Then he heard for the first time a recording by Plethyn singing the words of Myrddin ap Dafydd, 'Thicker than Water', a song inspired by his meeting with Bronwen in the church. He has pondered many times on the situation he found himself in, fighting against the country of his forefathers.

It was the saddest thing that my great grandfather had come from Wales to Patagonia to find peace to bring up his children, to keep up our religion, language and traditions - and then there I was fighting, as the song says, blood against blood.

After the war I focused on music, which acted like therapy and helped me to forget. But some things you can't forget. I was listening to the soldiers from Wales on the programme twenty years later, talking about digging trenches in the peat and the wet land out in the cold. That's exactly the same experience we had. Even today I can't put my foot down on mud without bad memories flooding back.

Since the conflict over three hundred of our soldiers have died, through suicide or from excessive drinking, as a result of the war. The war was a different experience for each one of us, depending on your background and state when you went into it. We should have had more psychological support. To my knowledge there isn't a single centre in Argentina specializing in treating mental health problems among ex-soldiers. We had no experience of war before the Malvinas, only of demonstrations, or of what the Government called rioting.

The question I go on asking about the war is 'For what?' It's unlikely there will ever be an answer. I strongly believe that the Malvinas should belong to Argentina - for historical, geographical, political and economic reasons. But when I think of the family of Mr Don Bonner, seven generations having lived on the islands, I think that they deserve to keep their way of life. Between the black and white there are many shades of grey. Before the war we were developing that centre ground well, with many young people from the islands studying in Argentina and liking the place. In the twenty years since the war we have gone back two or three generations.

What makes me sad is that what happened to me at twenty years old is still happening today to children in many parts of the world, and not just for three months. Though we can send people to the moon we can't talk to each other to resolve our problems here on earth.

5. MICHAEL JOHN GRIFFITH, SARN MELLTEYRN

It is a fine June evening, and Michael John Griffith is already preparing for winter. He is carefully stacking logs in a tidy pile at the side of his bungalow at the edge of Mynydd Rhiw. There is no breeze to stir the Red Dragon hanging on its pole between the house and Allt Coch Moel, and the view across the expanse of the Llŷn Peninsula is peaceful. In the centre there is Carn Fadryn, a rocky outcrop rising from the green fields. This is what Cynan yearned for in the turmoil of the First World War – 'Oh that a light breeze would come to soothe me/ From calm Carn Fadryn far away.' And this is the mountain that gave its name to Puerto Madryn in Patagonia, to which Milton Rhys and his fellow prisoners sailed home from their own Macedonia. But romanticizing any such links would have been the last thing on Michael John Griffith's mind as he fought the first battle of the Falklands war.

'I did know a bit about the history of the Welsh in Patagonia,' he says over a cup of tea inside, 'but I hadn't realised that Patagonia was a part of Argentina.'

> But if I had known at the time of the war that there were Welsh lads on the other side it wouldn't have made any difference. I was eighteen at the time, but anyone who's

been to war would say the same. You might as well not be there if you're going to be thinking 'I'm sure that lad over there has a brother or sister somewhere, or perhaps he's got a wife at home who's just had a baby.' In the same way, you can't be wondering if maybe his great grandfather came from Wales. It was war, and that was it.

Michael is a self-employed electrician. He lives in one of the quietest spots in Llŷn with his partner Heather and their busy, energetic little girl, Helena ('and as you can see, there's another on the way'). He says that his experience in the Falklands war has left him with no scars and that he rarely talks about it, although he's happy to do so if asked. His friends in Llŷn remember as well as he does that night the call to war came, while he was home on leave from the Navy during Easter 1982.

There was a gang of us at the *Lion* pub in Tudweiliog enjoying a pint and talking about girls when these two policemen came in. They pointed towards me and asked if I was Michael John Griffith. 'Yes' I said, and the place went totally quiet. 'Are you in the Marines?' 'Yes'. 'Come with us!' Mam and Dad had no phone in those days and the police had been sent to find me. Just before going to the *Lion* I had been talking to a friend in his farmyard and he told me that things were starting to get serious in the Falklands. 'Nothing will happen,' I said. 'Things like that don't happen these days.' Next minute, here was the policemen handing me a train warrant, and telling me to pack my things and get myself back to Bickleigh Barracks and 42 Commando.

Michael's luck, or misfortune, was that the group of marines he belonged to had been trained in exactly the type of warfare the strategists had forseen, not in the Falklands but on South Georgia, 800 miles further east. That island is a British dependency administered from Port Stanley, its terrain among the harshest in the world, the highest mountain standing almost three times the height of Snowdon, and the greater part of the island being covered with snow and ice for most of the year. It was there that the first signs emerged of the confrontation to come in the South Atlantic.

On the 19th of March 1982 the small group of British scientists based on South Georgia, members of the British Geological Survey, had some unexpected visitors. A party of Argentinian scrap dealers landed and said that they were there to dismantle and buy an old whale processing station in Leith. They were probably telling the truth. But along with the businessmen there were others dressed in military uniform, and they raised the Argentinian flag on the island.

On April 3rd more Argentinian soldiers landed by ship and three of them were killed in a skirmish with the handful of British Marines there before them. The British had little choice but to surrender. The War Cabinet in London decided that South Georgia had to be recaptured quickly, mainly for political reasons. It was thought necessary both to give a boost to the task force, which was on its way South, and to show the Argentinians that they meant business. Around 230 members of special forces were gathered for the task. The core of this group came from 42 Commando, and Michael John Griffith was one of them.

I had joined the Royal Marines at the end of 1980, a week before my seventeenth birthday – thinking pretty much that it would be a way of seeing the world. Nobody from my family had done anything like that, and I didn't know what to expect other than what I'd read in the pamphlets. We started at a training centre in Lympstone, Devon, and stayed there for six months. It was very interesting but terribly hard. There were 64 of us starting out and 28 left at the finish. But at the end I was accepted by 42 Commando.

Fighting in mountains, in snow and ice, is that unit's specialism. They spent every winter training in Norway, learning to ski, mountaineer and endure the cold.

We were in Narvik for three months, inside the Arctic Circle, and had a lot of laughs learning to ski. They taught us how to stand upright on skis, how to bend our knees, how to go downhill - everything but how to stop or turn! But by the end we could ski properly while carrying packs on our backs that were so heavy it took two men to lift them. We were there until the beginning of March, then we cleaned our guns and skis and stuff, put everything in the stores and went back home for Easter.

That was the holiday cut short by the two policemen in Tudweiliog. In no time everyone was back at barracks, their skis and guns out once again, under new orders.

Usually we came and went as we pleased - we didn't have to ask permission to leave the camp or anything like that. But from now on we weren't allowed to go further than ten minutes away from the place. We were on full operational alert and ready to move within 24 hours, unless anything happened on the political front. Every day new equipment arrived at the camp, shiny weapons from America, the most modern nylon ropes for abseiling down mountains. Anything anybody wanted was available. You only needed to ask.

'To your duties in the South Atlantic, quick march!'

That order from the commanding officer to the men of 42 Commando became one of the most famous of the war, but not all the men were marching in the same direction. Two of the unit's three companies got on buses to Southampton to sail to the Falklands on the *Canberra*, where the world and his wife would watch their departure on television. The exception was M Company, of which Michael was a member.

They marched us, a hundred and ten of us, to the gym at the barracks and warned us that everything we were told from now on was top secret. We were not to speak a word to anyone. We had been chosen to go to South Georgia with D Squadron of the SAS. The plan was to send a few of us with the SAS to South Georgia and give the Argentinians a good hiding there, so that they would recognize 'these guys mean business,' leave the Falklands and go home before anything worse happened. They were trying everything, I think, to prevent war.

We had one more night at the camp to prepare, getting our guns, grenade launchers and everything. And I remember phoning my mother from a kiosk and her saying 'We've seen that some of you are in Southampton...' They were filming the ships being loaded, trying to give the political dealings a nudge, showing that these lads were on their way and that we were serious. But nobody filmed us in case the other side realised that we were off to South Georgia then set out to defend the place better. I couldn't speak a word of this to Mam. I daren't do it.

The next day Michael and his group caught a bus to RAF Brize Norton before flying on to Ascension Island in the middle of the Atlantic, almost on the equator. This small island, British territory, became an important centre during the war.

A short time earlier I was in the Arctic Circle, then I'd been home to Pen Llŷn, and now I was on Ascension in terrific heat - all in ten days! It was quiet there when we arrived, no plane on the runway or anything. After we landed in the VC10 all these Hercules planes started coming in one after the other carrying all our gear. Helicopters picking stuff up in nets and flying it to ships out at sea. Everything started moving quickly all of a sudden.

The voyage from there to South Georgia lasted for a week and was an adventure in itself. There were four ships in the group, carrying between them six helicopters plus the soldiers, their kit and weapons. One of the ships was a tanker called the *Tidespring* carrying oil and water for the rest of the group. Michael was on board for the journey.

We went out to the ship on rafts, about twenty of us loaded on each one till we were almost disappearing under the water, while the helicopters carried all the gear. After reaching the ship, we were at it night and day loading. The helicopters landed at the back of the ship so all the weapons had to be kept at the front and they were very heavy. We formed human chains to pass the grenades and so on one to the next. I've never been in such a hot place, and we were all getting a bit light headed. We had to finish shifting everything forward before the ship could start.

A tanker like *Tidespring* isn't made to carry troops. Because it was so hot, fourteen of us slept out on the top deck. There was a little time to relax and study photos of South Georgia while they explained the plan to us. We trained during the day, abseiling off the bridge and so on. The conditions were good for about three days but then the weather began to change as we went further south. One night I woke to hear two or three bangs. The wind had risen and the waves were breaking over the top. We were in the middle of a storm, and all our camp beds got wet.

All this time the ships were moving together as fast as they could, and the water behind them was boiling. It was quite a sight to see this huge tanker supplying the other ships, the frigates and destroyers, with oil and water: the ships coming alongside each other, shooting a line across the bow of each one, and another line across the stern. Each line had different coloured flags to show when the ships were to go in or out, so that each one stayed completely in line as it was being filled.

The waves in the Atlantic can be enormous. We stopped in one place to practise getting into the inflatables at night. We put nets down the side of the ship and climbed down them carrying all our weapons. It wasn't stormy, but a big swell lifted our dinghies twelve to fifteen feet, so we had to time everything exactly. If the weather had been worse, that wouldn't have been a good place to be.

As the group neared South Georgia they received information that one of the Argentinian submarines was also on its way to the island: an old American sub called the *Santa*

Fe, powered by diesel and batteries. The belief was that she carried some soldiers from an Argentinian special forces unit, men who could make the job of recapturing the island much more difficult. The British group was now in even greater haste to reach the island ahead of them. A helicopter was sent out to search for the *Santa Fe*.

Because she was so old the submarine had to come up to the surface every once in a while to charge her batteries. The crew of a Wessex found her, fired a missile at the conning tower and put a hole in it. This slowed her down and prevented her from diving. By now we were only a bit too far out to be able to land, but the destroyer and the frigate were firing what they call NGS (naval gunfire support) at the Argentinians positioned in Grytviken Bay, and the SAS were beginning to land from *HMS Antrim*.

What happens with NGS is that the helicopter goes up and lets the ships know exactly where to fire - and they fired round after round as if they were trying to frighten the Argentinians. They knew that the *Santa Fe* hadn't arrived - she was still creeping her way in - and the SAS had landed behind them. I remember talking to some of the SAS boys afterwards. What they saw when they arrived was a football field, the only flat place there, and it's likely that there were anti-personnel mines, those little ones about the size of a saucer, everywhere all over. Then suddenly these SAS boys are all coming across it, the kind of thing the SAS does – they think 'we'll take a chance for the hell of it, I'll run across and if I lose a foot well there you go...'

Then we arrived, and you can imagine how the Argies felt seeing these shells coming closer and closer to them, snaking towards you and you knowing 'if we don't do something soon these will be landing right in my tea cup.' And the next thing was we saw a white flag being raised and we heard on the radio that they'd surrendered when the SAS reached them. And that was that, they put their weapons down.

A member of the *Santa Fe*'s crew was shot dead when one of the British soldiers thought he was trying to open a valve to sink the submarine. Apart from that no one on either side had shot anyone on the other in this first battle of the South Atlantic war. The next task was deciding what to do with the prisoners.

They had been put in different rooms at the British Geological Survey's station, but that wasn't built to keep POWs. Of course, they had all been frisked but nobody was tied up or anything. It was obvious that they didn't want to be there. They were conscripts and no one appeared to be looking for a fight. Across the island there were others as well saying by radio that they wanted to surrender. We guarded them, processed them, arranged food for them, somewhere to sleep and everything – with us working rotas, two hours at a time. Afterwards we got rid of them quite easily. I think we put them on an Argentinian ship. There was quite a sad look about them.

It was an anti-climax in a way. But we were there to do a job, which we did quite professionally. It's hard to give you a clear impression now of how things were there at the time. You don't see the weather, you don't see where we were in the middle of the mountains with the wind swirling and an iceberg as big as that barn over there going past. Nobody would really understand without having been there.

Another anti-climax was that we didn't go on to the Falklands. We'd been so busy preparing but now we were held back as a Quick Reaction Force – if something needed to be done in a hurry, or somebody had got into terrible trouble and a lot had been killed, we would have been called in to help them.

But we stayed on South Georgia all the while. After getting rid of the Argentinians there it was a very quiet war for us, but we couldn't leave in case they came back.

Michael's parents didn't hear from him until news broke that the Argentinians on the Falklands had surrendered and the war was at an end.

There was a satellite telephone on the *HMS Endurance* and they said that we'd be allowed to go over there and send a telegram or phone. When it was all over I went there to phone my grandmother's house. Even then I wasn't allowed to say where I was, only that I was fine.

In the end they sent the Scots Guards to take our place and a frigate type 31 came to take us back to Ascension, with helicopters there flying us to shore. By then we reckoned we had done a hell of a good job, and were feeling on top of the world. There were all kinds of things on Ascension by now, totally different from the quiet place it was when we first arrived. The post for us was still there, not having been sent on. I remember getting letters and a big cake. We were lying in the sun watching films, with plenty to drink. Everyone feeling the urge to let go, and no one was going to stop you.

Two nights there, and then they said a big welcome party was being organised for us at RAF St Mawgan in Cornwall. All our parents would be there and everybody would be making a fuss of us because we had liberated the first place among the islands - nice at the time but looking back, to tell the truth, we were being used to some extent.

At RAF St Mawgan, Mam and Dad, and all my family were there, lots of banners, all the dignitaries, the sound of cameras clicking and whirring. And that was that. We went back to camp with the guns and all the kit, cleaned and stored everything, exactly as if we had just finished in Norway. But in those six months I'd been from Narvik in the Arctic to the Antarctic, and back—and had a pint in the *Lion* on the way.

6. RONNIE GOUGH, EL BOLSON

No mountain was ever better named then El Piltriquitron. It rises straight and tall, twice the height of Snowdon, above the town of El Bolson in the Andes, its sculpted crest under heavy snow in the spring warmth of November. In the indigenous language it's name means 'mountain hanging from clouds'.

El Bolson is in Rio Negro, the region to the north of Y Wladfa, but Welsh is to be heard here as well. At the foot of the mountain sits a rustic guest house called *Rhona Hue*, 'Rhona's place'. Although Rhona is in her 80s and now lives in Bariloche, another hundred miles to the north, she still spends a lot of the time at the guest house helping her son, Ronnie. A short, lively, mischievous lady, Rhona speaks fluent Welsh. One of her great grandfathers was Michael D. Jones, who came up with the plan for Y Wladfa. Another was Lewis Jones, the pioneer who gave his name to Trelew. Rhona remembers Lewis Jones's wife and refers to her as 'Nain Fawr'. She has a book which belonged to Nain Fawr, Mrs Beeton's guide to house keeping.

Her son Ronnie doesn't speak Welsh though he wishes he could. His English is fluent and, as in the case of Milton Rhys, this influenced the work he was assigned to during the Malvinas War. Ronnie Gough's was the first voice the Kelpers heard speaking to them on the radio on April 2nd 1982.

Looking at him today, a kindly rather shy man who divides his time between the guest house and organising walking trips for visitors, it is hard to believe that Ronnie Gough was a senior military officer at the time of the dictatorship whose collapse was one of the few positive outcomes of the Malvinas war.

My father was born in Argentina but his family was English, on both sides. He worked as land manager for an English company which owned many large farms or 'estancias' here in Patagonia. Through that connection all of my primary and most of my secondary education took place at an English boarding school in Buenos Aires. I spoke the language fluently and they tried to expose us to a fair bit of English culture as well. Ironically I first learnt there too that the Malvinas belong to Argentina.

At 17 I went to the Naval College at Santiago, 60 kilometres from Buenos Aires. I was there for four years and graduated as a Midshipman. At the end of that period I went on a European voyage with one of the navy's training ships. I was in London for a while but didn't get a chance to look up my relatives in Wales. I've never been to Wales but I'm approaching 60 now and that's something I have to do before too long.

The time known as the 'dirty war', a very unfortunate period in our history as Argentinians, occurred during my career in the navy. It's not something anyone could be happy about and the consequences were appalling for both sides. We can have no pride in that part of our history. We did terrible things on both sides – I say 'we' because I was involved on the military side and we were fighting our fellow-countrymen. But you can't separate our history in Argentina then from what was happening in the rest of the world. It was the time of the Cold War, East against West, and we were part of that. One injustice is that some people on the other side are being regarded as heroes, even though they were doing hideous things as well. Thank God those days are over, but we are still paying the price for things that happened back then.

By the time of the Malvinas I was 35, a Lieutenant Commander, and second in command of a battalion of amphibious vehicles. They ran on tracks like tanks, each carrying 25 personnel from ship to land.

One morning in early January 1982, I got a call from the head of the Argentinian Marines, Admiral Busser. 'We've got to sort out all our vehicles,' he said, 'to go on manoeuvres with the Army.' I asked him how many men we needed to land. 'Five hundred,' he said. 'but this is only an exercise.' So we set about it repairing and renovating all the vehicles.

January is mid-summer for us, and during that month I was responsible for the battalion because the usual commander was on holiday. Then I went on holiday myself, and when I got back in February the situation looked much more serious. I read the newspapers and tried to get some sense of what was going on. I was sure that we were going on quite a critical exercise with the army. Then the time came to leave Puerto Belgrano, where the naval ships are normally at anchor. The preparation was over and we were sailing for the Malvinas.

We were at sea for five or six days, caught up in a terrible storm. But the second of April was fine and the storm had calmed. I thought at this time that I would be responsible for the landing craft during the invasion. But because I spoke English I was moved to another assignment, communicating with the people of the islands. That could entail dealing with some of those responsible for the radio station – the British Royal Marines who were on the island and the islanders who had received some training for the Falkland Islands Local Defence Force. It was my voice the islanders heard reading the communiqués broadcast by radio.

A group of us arrived in Puerto Argentino by helicopter at around seven o'clock in the morning. We weren't the first to get there and the airfield was full of tractors and landrovers that would have made it impossible for any of our planes to land.

I was supposed to run towards the Governor, Rex Hunt's house. The plan was for us to capture it, and Rex Hunt was to be told in English what to do. But as often happens with military matters, things didn't turn out as planned. The Royal Marine Corps had been positioned in another part of the island, at Moody Brook, and it was there that we expected most of the fighting to take place. But the English were thinking differently. Their priority was to defend the Governor's house as he was the Queen's representative on the island.

My friend Pedro Giachino was in charge of a group stationed in front of the Governor's house, the building to be seized at the appointed time. Nothing seemed to be happening and he was losing patience. He ran towards the house himself since there seemed to be no one there. But most of the British Marines, around 30 in all, were in there. So as he rushed across the open ground towards the house he was shot. Most of the Marines were taken prisoner. But Pedro Giachino was badly wounded and eventually died.

At that moment I was about a mile from Puerto

Argentino on the other side of the town. After landing the helicopter we had taken a landrover and driven towards the town. But there were two or three Marines shooting at us, stopping us from getting there. By the time I reached Government House it was obvious that there had been fighting. As I headed for the house another landrover drove across my path. Somebody took a picture of the two landrovers and it was published in a magazine in Argentina. I realised afterwards that the other landrover was taking my great friend Pedro to the hospital.

Captain Pedro Giachino became a legendary figure in Argentina. He is remembered as the first to lose his life in the Malvinas war, though some English accounts suggest that up to five Argentinians died in the first battle. But Giachino commanded the attack, and he died leading his men bravely if impulsively. He is compared with Colonel H. Jones VC, who was killed in similar circumstances at the battle of Goose Green. It is more than likely that Pedro Giachino was one of the men the nurse Bronwen Williams helped, trying to save his life at the hospital. It is as a friend rather than a hero that Ronnie Gough remembers him:

Pedro was someone everybody took to straight away. He was a big man, very amusing, also brave – always leading from the front. I met him when we both went to the military academy in 1964, and we kept in touch through the years. I remember a chat we had at headquarters when we were getting ready. 'El Ingles,' he said - 'the Englishman' was my nickname with my friends because I spoke the language – 'El Ingles, here we are at last , we are on our way, once and for all!' Two or three times earlier in our careers we had been close to going to war with Chile but were turned back at the last minute. That was frustrating, and Pedro was happy that we were not turning back this time. I agreed. We were irresponsible, but full of idealism at that time about defending our country and so on.

We had received unequivocal orders not to put ourselves in danger. And I heard from some of the men Pedro was commanding that he had said the same thing to them: 'Nothing rash, everything logical, no risks.' But when it came to the matter of taking Government House he was the first to rush in. He was wearing a bulletproof jacket but was hit in the leg, severing the main vein.

By the time Ronnie reached the Governor's house, the main orders had changed. His military superior was there before him and Ronnie didn't see the Governor Rex Hunt.

I was ordered to take all the members of the Falkland Islands Local Defence Force together to a gym and, from there, back to their own homes. Meanwhile some of our group went to take over the radio station. By the time I got there Patrick Watts, who ran the station, was extremely nervous. I had with me a young officer, a midshipman, who wasn't very savvy. Like many youngsters he saw everything in black and white. So I had to send the midshipman out, then I said to Patrick Watts that I'd be going home, that I'd come back the next day and see what we could do. I talked to another man there at the radio station – I don't remember his name but I think he was Australian. 'Ronnie,' he said, 'You've got no idea what will be happening from now on.' The suggestion was that the British Government would be sending their armed forces to throw us out of the islands, and of course his prediction was completely true.

My job was to read the communiqués to let people know what was happening. A friend of mine has kept a recording of some of them but I wouldn't much want to listen to it by now.

There are scripts of the broadcasts and this was one of the first:

At this historic highly important moment for us all, it is my pleasure to greet the people of the Malvinas and exhort you to co-operate with the new authorities by complying with all the instructions that will be given through oral and written communiqués, in order to facilitate the normal life of the entire population.

These words are attributed to Osvaldo Jorge Garcia, who had been given the title ' The Governor of the Islas Malvinas, Georgia del Sur and Sandwich del Sur'. But it's probably the voice of Ronnie Gough that was heard broadcasting the message.

I would chat on the phone with some islanders who weren't happy with things they had heard on the radio, nothing particularly important. I also remember a couple from England who were visiting and wanted to know how they could get away. My English was better than it is these days and they couldn't believe that they were talking to an Argentinian. It's these little things that have stuck in my memory, nothing of great significance at all concerning the war.

One funny thing happened, to do with a major in our army. He told me to put out a message on the radio that the islanders, from now on, had to drive on the right, as we did in South America. That was the order that had come from the General, he said. I couldn't believe I was getting an instruction like that. I said I had no intention of giving the islanders such a stupid order, that there were more important things to worry about. That happened at around midnight. Next morning the major came round and asked if I had made the announcement, saying that the General himself was behind the decision. I said that I hadn't broadcast the order and didn't intend to. By this point I had informed my own superior in the navy about it, and his reaction was to laugh about it. Remember it was us, the Argentinian Marines, who were responsible for the first landing, but by this time we had an Army General above us. I never saw that Major again afterwards, and I don't know whether they changed things later about which side of the road the traffic was supposed to drive on.

But that afternoon I was driving around the island in the landrover. I was on the right, where I was used to driving, and the islanders, or 'Kelpers', were of course still driving on the left. As I rounded a corner I came face to face with another landrover on my side, driving straight at me. The driver was a member of the Falkland Islands Defence Force, and I had just freed him that morning. We recognized each other and both laughed about it. But we were within seconds of an accident. I started thinking that perhaps the General was right, and I should have issued that order after all!

It was only during the first attack that Ronnie Gough was on the islands. His time there ended after 72 hours.

Late one night, or very early in the morning, we were put on a plane and taken to Tierra del Fuego, the southernmost part of Patagonia. Our belief at the time was that a small crew of Argentinian soldiers would stay on the islands, the fighting would end, to be replaced by a diplomatic wrangle. After the first shock Britain would show better leadership on the subject of the Malvinas, and the politicians would come to some agreement. But that's not how things turned out of course.

I was on the islands during the 'good' part of the war, and gone before the real fighting started. One day when I was supervising my unit in Tierra del Fuego, I saw an old friend I had known since naval training. He was a pilot by now. We had dinner together. The next day he went out on an attack over the Malvinas, and after failing to find a target he came back with a full load of bombs. There was ice on the runway, the plane started to skid, he jumped, hit the ground and was killed immediately. Afterwards the plane straightened out on its own and kept going till it came to a stop with no damage. That pilot and Pedro Giachino where the only friends I lost during the war.

I'm still completely clear in my own mind that Argentina's claim to the islands is legitimate. But the way we set about winning them wasn't right. We did exactly what Mrs Thatcher wanted us to do, and that cost both sides dearly.

One good thing that came out of it was to make Argentinians begin to appreciate democracy. People were fed up with military rule and we were kicked out of power. It's a shame that we had to go through the 'dirty war' and the Malvinas war before that happened. Thank God the Argentinian people will never want to be ruled by the military again and, more importantly, the military has no wish to be in charge. For twenty years military people have seen themselves more as part of the problem then than part of the solution, and I hope this recognition continues.

7. HOWARD JONES, Y FELINHELI

On the four fingers of his left hand are tattoos of the letters J O S K – for 'Joskins', the nickname Bangor children gave to boys from the mountains. For some reason they regarded the nearby seaside village of Y Felinheli (or Port Dinorwic) as also being in the mountains. That's how Richard Howard came to be 'Joskin' at school, a name later resurrected in the Welsh Guards. He was introduced to me as Howard, although some of his friends at the pub in Bangor where we met to talk called him Rich.

Like his friend Wil Howarth, who tells his story in chapter 9, Howard stayed in the Army for years after the Falklands war - ending his career, again like Wil, as a Sergeant in the Recruiting Office in Bangor. They both say that one of the reasons they got work there was because they could speak Welsh.

Howard left the Army in April 1988, 'five years this Sunday,' and since then has worked as a safety officer and handyman at the government benefits office in Caernarfon – work, according to some of his stories, that can be almost as dangerous as being in the Army. His greatest pleasure in life is fishing. He likes nothing better than taking time off in his boat on the Menai Straits. Unlike Wil, Howard has no difficulty relaxing and staying calm. He says that the Falklands had no great lasting effect on him. There was one difference between them though: Howard was on land while Wil and some of his other friends were on the *Galahad*.

I went to Felin School first then Deiniol School in Bangor, but I left there at 15 and went to work at the meat place in Felin, the 'Laughing Pig' as we called it. I was there for about two years and I had four or five jobs after that. I couldn't settle anywhere. I was going out with a girl from Caernarfon and, to tell the truth, that was stopping me from joining the Army as I wanted to. I had a cousin in the Army and I fancied going, but I didn't because of the girl. Then we split up and that's when I joined. I didn't last long the first time, only a week or two, because she was phoning me all the time and I came out for a year. We separated for good then, and I said 'OK I'm going this time' and that's what happened. I joined the Army and there I stayed for 23 years and 265 days.

I was a bad lad at first, always in trouble with the Army. I was also in trouble before then, to tell the truth, what with fighting in Caernarfon and other things. The Magistrate said to me in court that if I came up before him again I was going to jail. But I didn't go back, I joined the Army. What happened then when I was in trouble was that the police would say 'Oh, you're a soldier. We'll take you back to camp and they'll deal with you there.' You know what it's like, people drinking, this and that, just a bit of fighting isn't it? Every soldier's done it some time I'm sure – fighting with people on the street. That's how they get their training.

When I first joined the Guards I was the only recruit there from North Wales. They called me Jonesy at that time, but when I landed in the Regiment there were lads from Bangor there, and that's where they started calling me Joskin. So Josk I remained then in the Army. It stuck with me for the 23 years and 265 days.

It wasn't long before he realised that people were being killed in the Army, and without having to go to war for that to happen. He was at one of the Guildford pubs attacked during the IRA bombings in 1975.

You couldn't go home during the first five weeks of training, but in the third week you were allowed out for a drink, and to stay out until ten o'clock at night. One night a gang of us went to Woking, and it was boring there, so we went on to Guildford. We were walking up towards this pub, the *Horse and Groom*, the best place they said, and there were people running down the street towards us telling us not to go there, that it had been blown up. That didn't mean a thing to us. We weren't going to be killed after only being in the Army for three weeks. So we went on to this other place, the *Seven Stars*. We walked in, ordered a pint, and Bang! That place went up as well, with me inside! I wasn't hurt, but I had a leather coat which was slashed by the broken glass, and I got knocked out.

As I walked out of the *Seven Stars* I could see fish swimming down the road. I was thinking 'Christ I must be seeing things'. But when I reached the end of the road people were grabbing hold of us because we were dizzy, and asking if we were drunk. 'No,' we said, and an ambulance took us to hospital where they checked us over before returning us to camp and the medical centre, where we stayed overnight. After all that I got to know more about those fish. Across the road from the *Seven Stars* there was an aquarium. The explosion had smashed it open, setting the water and the fish flowing down the road. And there was I imagining that I was seeing things!

Two Scots Guards in the same platoon as me were killed by the bomb. A lot of lads left the Army after that. But I stayed. A week after the bomb we started training again and there were people collapsing on the square, suffering from delayed shock. I got £50 from the Guildford Bomb Fund, a lot of money in 1975.

Howard was promoted to Lance Corporal while stationed in Berlin in 1978, then moved back to Surrey where he stayed for four years. During that time he met his wife, Sarah. 'That's when I started getting some sense. From day one she sorted me out. I haven't been in any trouble since then.' Another period in Germany came next, near to what had been the location of Belsen concentration camp. Then back to Pirbright in Surrey, where the couple were married in February 1982. Within another two months Howard was on his way to war in the South Atlantic.

I was a Lance Corporal then for the second time, having lost my stripes once. I knew nothing of the Falklands, and when I first heard the name I thought they must have been some islands up in Scotland. But I got to know, of course, that they're much further away. They taught us a lot during training before heading down and on the *QE2* we were shown slides of the rock rivers there - like rivers but full of boulders.

On the night I was leaving we were in bed, my missus asleep beside me, and I was wondering 'Am I going to wake her, or what?' And I didn't. I slipped out of bed, down the stairs, clothes on and out of the door. It was about half past five in the morning. Down then on the bus from Pirbright to Southampton and onto the QE2.

We knew when we were about half way there that the war was going to happen. Some of the Marines had already arrived at the islands, and the *Belgrano* had been sunk. When we trained on the QE2 what we were doing was firing from the back of the ship at plastic bags in the water using live ammunition, exactly as you see them doing training now for Iraq. You knew you were going to war.

We stopped in two places on the way, in Freetown, Sierra Leone, and then in South Georgia. There we saw the submarine they had attacked, and the old whaling station where it had all started. The QE2 went no further. We were transferred to the *Canberra* and got off finally on to the jetty at San Carlos.

I was in the reconnaissance platoon. We stayed two or three miles from San Carlos, digging trenches, sleeping the night, then packing our kit and moving on. Half the platoon went off by helicopter somewhere and they were supposed to return to fetch us, but they didn't come. We started walking then up some mountain following the route the Paras had taken for about five or six miles along a track. After that they told us that something had happened and we had to turn back towards San Carlos. There we boarded *HMS Fearless* and she took us round to a beach in Fitzroy Bay. Our crew was the first to go ashore by landing craft because we were supposed to do a recce of the place. We walked on then about four or five miles to some old quarry to wait.

We didn't know anything about what had happened to the rest of the battalion. Nobody said much to us. It got light, it got dark, and the day after we heard that the lads were coming on another ship. When we were in the quarry it was 'Air Warning Red', because they were expecting planes to come across. We were on standby all the time. Half an hour's rest, then standby again. We heard the planes coming across and bombs going off and saw smoke rising, but we couldn't see any ships or anything, nothing but smoke. From where we were in the quarry a kind of small valley ran down to the beach. And the planes were coming down the estuary to hit the Galahad where our friends were. They were no more than about thirty feet above our heads. We could see the pilots' faces clearly. There was a machine gun platoon ahead of us shooting at them, and us shooting as best we could, then the Gurkhas and another platoon of Welsh Guards were also shooting at them but they kept on going through everything. We could see bits coming off them and perhaps some of them did come down, but we didn't see any.

Afterwards when these planes had gone we could see this thick smoke again and started to find out what had happened. 'The boys are all on the ships and they've been hit,' they said to us. It made things worse that one or two of our lads had brothers on the *Galahad*. One boy from Liverpool who was with us, in the machine gun platoon, had two brothers on the *Galahad*, but luckily they came off alright.

The British plan was to capture a string of mountains surrounding Port Stanley and clear the path for an attack on the town itself. Howard Jones was transferred to the Commando platoon which was preparing the way for an attack on Mount Harriet.

Our job was doing the reconnaissance. We walked from

the quarry over towards Mount Harriet and marked out a start line about 300 metres from where we knew the Argentinian forward positions were. Then when the Marines arrived we could tell them exactly where to go straight up the mountain, and show them where we knew there were Argentinians.

One night the Marines had gone up the mountain, we had started going up, we stopped in one place just for a minute, and suddenly there was the firing and all sorts starting up. One of the boys shouts 'Hey, there's someone running towards us here!' So we start asking each other what 'Halt' is in Spanish, and none of us can remember even though they'd taught us on the ship on the way down. 'Fuck it, watch this,' one of the lads said. 'HALT!' he shouted, and this boy stopped straight off with his hands up in the air. He had understood very well. He was our prisoner for the night and he shared his fags with us. He had plenty of fags, and we didn't have any.

After everything settled and the Marines had gone up the mountain, we walked back down, and these Argentinians started shooting at us. We fired about 7,000 rounds between eight of us, and they didn't shoot again. We went back to the rest of the platoon. We were just settling down to sleep when we got a message that there were helicopters on the way to pick us up, that the Argentinians had run away and that we should try to catch them before they settled in again. Then there were a load of helicopters coming in. I've never seen so many before all together - picking us all up and dropping us on the path about two miles away from Sapper Hill, the mountain that looks down on Port Stanley. We started moving then towards Sapper Hill. We were supposed to attack it. You could see them beginning to run, but one or two of them started shooting at our front column, though far away from where I was. One or two of our crew were killed there. By the time we reached Sapper Hill it was all over. There were bodies, some of them in a hell of a mess. I remember one with his head off, and still no blood to be seen. But I didn't see as much of that kind of thing as a lot of the other boys did. By the time I reached Stanley the war had been over for three days and the bodies buried.

The soldiers' job then was to clear up the mess on the streets. After sleeping for a few nights in sheds in Fitzroy, Howard Jones and his crew were moved into houses in Stanley where the Argentinians had stayed and the original inhabitants had not yet returned.

We painted the house where we were staying. The water system wasn't working but one of our lads who'd been a plumber fixed it and then we could have a bath. There was one of those big peat-burning ovens there, which was blocked, but we managed to mend that as well. Then we bought some lamb from the locals and had a good feed. The house was like new by the time the people who lived there moved back in.

But on our last day in Stanley, we were at it cooking half a lamb with another hour or so's cooking still to go, and a nice smell about the place, when our boss came and said 'Pack your kit, we're going.' 'What, are we heading home?' we said. 'No, we're going to Argentina.' 'What?' We had no idea what was going on, but we were about to escort the prisoners on their way home. We packed all our stuff, but we made sure to take our time so that the meat was well cooked. I was walking down the road with a rucksack, a suitcase, this and that, with half a leg of lamb in my other hand, eating it as I went.

Down to the jetty in Port Stanley then, and onto the small boat taking us out to the ship. She was an old British Rail ferry. It was on her that we took the POWs, on what they called tank decks but were really car decks. The conscripts and other ranks were all on these decks, but the officers could sleep in cabins. Our job was to look after these, make sure they were fed, take them for a daily shower and make sure they weren't being naughty boys. We still carried guns until they got off the ship at Puerto Madryn.

At one place in the upper part of the ship there was a wide corridor with a chair outside a cabin door. There was always a guard sitting on that chair, on what we called stags, or stints lasting two hours. I did three or four stags there and it was obvious that someone important was inside that cabin because the bosses told me 'When he comes out, don't point a gun at him.' That's when I understood that General Menendez was in there. I'd never seen the bloke before, but suddenly two men came out. One of them was a giant, a huge man, and I thought, 'Jesus, no wonder this bloke's a general.' By his side was this little bloke, who looked a bit soft to me. But afterwards I learned that he was Menendez. And that the big bloke was his aide or something.

Howard didn't realise at the time that Puerto Madryn, where the prisoners were being taken, was in the Welsh part of Patagonia, but he says that he came across one prisoner on the ship who spoke a certain amount of Welsh.

There was this corridor between the cabins which had

been blocked at both ends, with me and another boy guarding each end with machine guns. We were speaking Welsh and this Argentinian officer came out of his cabin and said something to us in Welsh. At the time, I had to say to him 'I don't care, get back in your cabin.' We weren't supposed to talk to them, except to tell them where to go, and what to do. Perhaps he wouldn't have been able to have a proper chat with us in Welsh, but it would have been nice to know what he could say.

A harbour wall in the middle of nowhere was where they got off in Puerto Madryn. I remember some of them were wearing the *Belgrano* uniform, and white sailor's hats with *Belgrano* written on them, but I don't know if they had been on the ship. We weren't there for long. Some of them were wounded and went straight into ambulances. As soon as they were all off, we were on our way heading back to Port Stanley. There the rest of the Regiment joined us on board the ship, and off we went to Ascension Island. It was very rough in the South Atlantic on a British Rail ferry, but things improved as we got nearer the equator. I slept for about four days.

Twenty years later Howard and his friend Wil Howarth were back in the Falklands being filmed for *Y Byd ar Bedwar* with Tweli Griffiths. Howard was glad of that opportunity.

It was good to see the place again. I was fine with that, but I felt for Wil, as he'd been on the *Galahad*. I didn't know how he would feel about visiting Fitzroy and Bluff Cove and places like that. But he handled it fine, judging by what I saw, and yes, we did enjoy ourselves. When our plane landed, Patrick Watts was waiting for us. He was that bloke who was in the radio station when the

Argentinians first landed – the one who told them to put their guns down and that he wasn't going anywhere. It was nice to see the people of Port Stanley, and to see them so happy. And to tell you the truth, we didn't have to spend anything while we were there.

We saw some of the shoes, or thin plimsolls, the Argentinian conscripts wore, still there on the island stuck in the ground. It was terribly cold for them there. We had been trained over the years. I'd been in the Army for seven years by that time and I had trained in hot places like Kenya, and in the Baltic where the wind came in from every direction with rain and snow and the cold all the time. That training taught you how to keep yourself alive and to make sure you didn't get hypothermia and the like.

Was it worth going to war over the islands? Howard thinks before answering.

The islanders say yes, it was worth it. But thinking of the friends I lost, no, it wasn't. I lost a lot of my friends on the *Galahad*. It wasn't worth it. It would have been easier and cost less to get hold of everybody and move them back to this country and let them live here. OK, they feel differently of course - that's their country, over there.

Being in the Falklands war didn't have much effect on me, although my wife wouldn't agree. For around six months I couldn't settle down or sleep. In the morning the missus would be sleeping downstairs, and I'd be asking what was the matter. 'You were at it again last night, tossing and turning and hitting the pillow,' she'd say. I don't remember anything, of course. I was asleep. But after six months or so things got better. The only other thing that happened was that I lost all feeling in my fingers because the cold had affected them. I couldn't pick a penny up off the table. That lasted about six months too, then the feeling came back. But I still struggle when the weather's cold. I only go fishing once a month in winter now because of that. But I fish every day in summer.

(From top left, clockwise) Denzil Connick, on the right of the
picture, at the ceremony to place the South Atlantic torch at the
Cenotaph in London (photo: *SAMA82*); Denzil at his office in
Pontllanfraith, where he manages *SAMA82*, an organization for
Falklands ex-combatants on the British side; the Malvinas Memorial
in Buenos Aires, naming the 650 Argentinians who died.

(From top left, clockwise) Milton
Rhys from Trelew; the Malvinas war
memorial near his home; Bronwen
Douse (previously Williams); and
the church in Port Stanley where the two met in 1982.

(Above) Bronwen nursing in Port Stanley and with a group of her friends outside the Nurses' Home. She is on the left in the front row. The fourth from the left is Susan Whitley from Llandrindod, one of the 3 islanders killed in the war.
(Below) Port Stanley in 2002 (photo: Howard Jones)

(Above) Former Welsh Guard Wil Howarth, who was rescued from the flames of the *Sir Galahad*, back in Port Stanley in 2002.
He visited the islands with his friend Howard Jones (Middle).
(Below) The welcome from the people of Amlwch for Wil Howarth at the end of the war – and the luxurious menu on the *QE2*, which was available to the soldiers for a few days.

Dinner

SELECTED MENU

Crayfish Cocktail, Russian Dressing

Brandied Crabflake Bisque

Paupiette of Beef Princesse
Whole Green Beans
Parslied Potatoes

Hungarian Log

Coffee

Julio Oscar Gibbon, still a soldier in Esquel in 2002. Argentina's right to sovereignty over the Malvinas proclaimed in a street name in Trevelin and over the mouth of a tunnel in Gaiman.

(Above) Michael John Griffith at his home in Llŷn, near Carn Fadryn, which gave its name to Puerto Madryn, where the Welsh language still lives on.

(Middle) A plaque commemorating the first Welsh landing in 1865.

(Below) Michael at the grave of the explorer Shackleton on South Georgia in 1982.

Two men from Dolavon, now living in Trelew, who were in the Malvinas throughout the war: (from the upper left) Horacio Kent and Carlos Eduardo Apiwan, who received the certificate above for his service. (Right) the memorial for Lewis Jones, after whom Trelew was named.

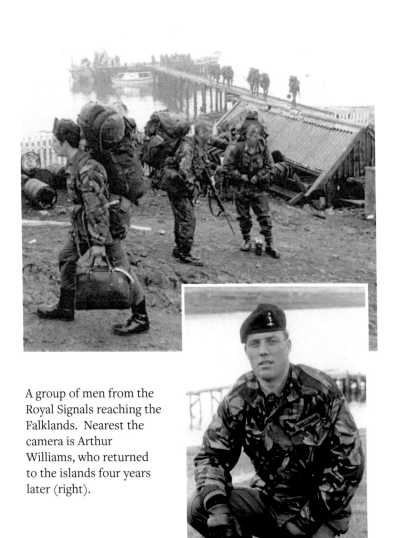

A group of men from the Royal Signals reaching the Falklands. Nearest the camera is Arthur Williams, who returned to the islands four years later (right).

Ronnie Gough (left) was only on the islands for a few days but his voice became familiar to the locals on 'Radio Malvinas'. By 2002 he ran a guest house in the mountains in El Bolson with the help of his mother Rhona (below), a great-granddaughter of both Michael D. Jones and Lewis Jones.

This was a dark period in the history of the Argentinian Welsh community even when not directly affected by the fighting. From the top left, clockwise: Irma Hughes de Jones, Gaiman; Vali James de Irianni, Buenos Aires; Iris Spannaus, Buenos Aires; Rini Griffith, Esquel.

Comodoro Rivadavia was one of Argentina's most important military centres, a cause for concern among the inhabitants. John Benjamin Lewis (above), Lila Hughes de Gastaldi and Walter Ariel Brooks – who was a child at the time of the war and now lives in Cardiff. (Right) The hospital in Comdoro Rivadavia where soldiers wounded in the Malvinas were treated, and where many parents looked in vain for their lost sons.

Welshness in the Chubut Valley: Tomi Davies 'Hyde Park', aged 95; and four buildings, including the *Tŷ Gwyn* guest house where the author stayed when in Gaiman in 2002.

Above – a Welshman in Argentina: Russell Isaac interviewing Argentinian General Reynaldo Bignone, for the programme *Y Dydd* in April 1982. Shortly afterwards Russell was arrested on suspicion of spying.

Right – an Argentinian in Wales: Elvey MacDonald, whose mother was interrogated at Heathrow Airport for the same reason.

Two adventurers in one family. Thomas Tegai Awstin is the first name on the *Mimosa* memorial in Puerto Madryn, where he landed at 11 years old. And the name of his great grandson, Ricardo Andres Austin, is on the Malvinas War memorial in Buenos Aires. Thomas Awstin became one of the pillars of Welsh community life in Cwm Hyfryd, and his family is still there. Here is the Welsh Centre

in Esquel (middle) and Jorge Austin (right) who works there.

Ricardo Andres Austin (left, and above on the way to war with his battalion) was killed in the battle of Darwin and Goose Green.
It was twenty years before his mother Celinde (below) received the official report on his death.

Tom and Eileen Roberts from Llanberis who lost their son, Raymond, on the *HMS Ardent*.
(Below) John Raymond Roberts as a child, and in naval uniform.

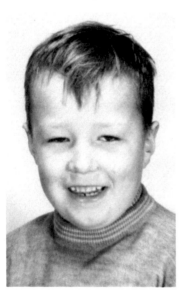

8. CARLOS EDUARDO APIWAN, TRELEW

I looked many times through the official list of Argentinian ex-soldiers who served in the Malvinas, searching for names that sounded Welsh, and missed the name Carlos Eduardo Apiwan. It took the sharp eye of a Gaiman resident to notice it and recognize that the 'ap' and the 'Iwan' had got stuck together somewhere down the generations. Carlos Eduardo was listed under the Trelew area. But who was he? Was he descended from Llwyd ap Iwan, the son of Michael D. Jones? Did he speak Welsh? If you're in Gaiman and involved in any dilemma to do with Welsh life, the usual advice is 'Ask Luned!'

It became apparent that Luned Gonzalez, the lively ex-headmistress and matriarch of Y Wladfa's Welsh community, had a knack for detective work. As Llwyd ap Iwan's granddaughter, she knew that the ap Iwan whose trail we were on was not of that lineage. But she did know of a minister who emigrated from Wales to Y Wladfa and followed the example of Michael D. Jones in adapting the Welsh form for his children's surname, changing it from Jones to ap Iwan. She was sure that Carlos Eduardo was a descendant of that Jones. Two or three telephone calls later and Luned the detective had also established that Señor Apiwan was a policeman.

Then she started phoning Trelew's police stations, and

there are quite a few of those in a city of a hundred thousand people. In no time she reached the right station and got hold of a home telephone number for Constable Apiwan, who wasn't on duty that afternoon. I doubted if there would be a way of persuading a policeman to talk about a war he was involved in twenty years earlier, and that with a stranger from the Old Country, which was also in the land of the 'enemy'. 'The worst he can do is say "No",' said Luned, picking up the phone. But he didn't. Not only was he happy to talk but he also offered to come over to meet us at Luned's house in Gaiman, to save us a journey.

But he didn't arrive at the time arranged. Half an hour later there was still no sign of him. Had he lost his way, forgotten, changed his mind, or perhaps had advice from his superiors not to discuss the war? No one was answering the phone at his home, and after about an hour I went back to my hotel disappointed. My days in Gaiman were coming to an end and it was unlikely there would be a second opportunity.

But Luned isn't one to give up easily. She called my hotel to say that she had managed to contact Señor Apiwan, who had explained. He was a member of the Trelew drug squad and had been called out urgently that afternoon to Puerto Madryn on police business. Madryn is an hour's journey from Trelew and he had only just got back, but we were welcome to come to his house. A policeman with the name ap Iwan heading from Trelew to Puerto Madryn on a drugs case 137 years after the *Mimosa* . . . it's a strange world.

So finally Luned and I were driving in her car through the labyrinth of Trelew's back streets until we reached a house with a high gate in front of it. The policeman came to the door with a welcoming smile, but before letting us in he had to lead two fierce looking wolfhounds to a place where we would be out of their reach.

He had no Welsh and I don't speak Spanish but Luned was in her element translating. He explained that his wife kept a shop in a street nearby selling a little of everything, staying open till late at night so that they could save money for home improvements. They had four children and we got to meet the two youngest, Alexa aged eight and Jimena who was twenty months old. They were, like their father, of dark complexion and any physical trace of the Welsh lineage had long disappeared. Framed on the wall was a certificate acknowleging his service in the Malvinas war.

I don't know anything about my father's family in Wales, only that some of them arrived here on the ship. I know of course that my surname comes from Wales. There's some talk that an uncle of my father's was born on the ship on the way across.

My family was a hundred percent Welsh on my father's side and a hundred percent Spanish on my mother's. Hughes was my grandmother's surname before she married and became ap Iwan. I had an uncle named Edward ap Iwan. I was named Eduard after him. I was born in Dolavon and went to primary school there. I didn't go to secondary school because there was only a private one in the area. So after leaving school I went to help my father at home on the farm. There I stayed until I got the call-up to do military service.

My dad and mum still live in Dolavon. They don't live on the farm any more but my father still goes there, back and forth. He is 72 years old. He can't speak Welsh any more by now but he could when he was young. He would speak Welsh with his mother but after she died he no longer got to use the language. My aunts, the Hugheses, all spoke Welsh.

I was aged nineteen and one day when the war started in the Malvinas. April the first is my birthday and the war started on the second, in 1982. Four months earlier I had started my military service. I was a member of Regiment 8 in Comodoro Rivadavia.

When they told us we were going to war in the Malvinas we were all delighted. There was a lot of rejoicing because we had been hearing since primary school how the islands had been stolen from us. But everything changed after we got there. The weather and everything else was against us. We reached Puerto Argentino by Hercules military aircraft on the morning of April the fourth.

I had never thought much about the fact that I came from a Welsh background. But my friends pulled my leg during the war. 'You've got a Welsh name,' they said. 'Nothing will be happening to you!'

I was responsible for a unit that was watching the shore, in case British soldiers landed. We received messages all the time, that the landing would be happening here, or over there, so we were being moved often from place to place. At least we weren't having to sleep in holes in the ground, like the soldiers who were stationed in one place. We slept in tents, army tents.

The weather was very cold - one day it was snowing then freezing. We had ordinary army clothing, nothing for the cold weather, and ordinary rubber shoes because there was so much water in the ground close to the surface. We were in those clothes for the three months. If we got wet we would try to dry the clothes on our bodies in the tent, and this was happening all the time. We weren't getting half enough food either.

We only saw the people who lived on the island from

a distance. But there was no trouble at all. They seemed to be very polite people.

We were mostly wandering around Puerto Argentino, but we would be moved sometimes to other areas where there was fighting. They would be shooting at us and we would be shooting at them non-stop every day. For two months we'd be attacked as well by the ships, planes and helicopters. One of my best friends was killed. I shared a tent with him when we were in training in Comodoro. Not a day passed without shooting, not one day of peace. We felt half way between dead and alive. That's how things were from the fourth of April till I was taken prisoner. That happened in Bahia Falk, Puerto Riveros, at the end of the fighting. There are a lot of things I don't remember - they were such tough experiences.

When we were taken prisoner we stayed on the island one more night. Until that moment it was as if we didn't understand properly what was happening. After that they took us away from there in a helicopter to a ship. About that time the armistice was being signed but we didn't know anything about it until a few hours beforehand. Until then we believed we were winning the war. The message our officers were giving us was that everything was under control. That was why it was such a shock when we heard that it wasn't true.

We were treated well as prisoners. Nobody attacked us physically at all, at least not where I was. The only thing that terrified us was being around foreigners speaking a different language and us not able to understand a word.

We had no idea where we were going, but when we were on the little boat taking us out to the ship a British soldier who spoke Spanish came up to us and said that a peace treaty had been signed and we were going back home to Argentina. We were taken to a ship, I believe she was called the *Norland*, and one morning we reached Puerto Madryn. We had no idea of the time during the voyage. We were shut in cabins, two or three per cabin and no going outside except to the toilet. They'd bring food to us in the cabins.

Some of the boys have suffered terribly after the experience. Personally, thank God, I haven't suffered much. For about the first three months after coming home I couldn't rest properly because I was still feeling anxiety. Since then I believe I've been fine, physically and mentally.

They kept me in the army for two months after the war but I wasn't doing much work. They wanted the doctors to treat us and make sure we were in good shape. Afterwards I worked in a factory , then I did building work, until I went on a course to join the police. That was when I was 24 years old.

I know about one boy from a Welsh background who was killed in the war. I got to know Andres Austin before the war. He was from the Andes and came to work for a while in Trelew, in a petrol station I think. We got to know each other through another lad who was a friend of both of us. Andres was 18 at the time and I was 17. We'd go to dances together. He was a quiet boy and very good company. The fact that we were both of Welsh blood wasn't something we talked about much - it felt natural to us, something we'd both always lived with. But other people would pull our legs sometimes seeing that both of us had Welsh names, Apiwan and Austin. That's common in Patagonia, people who have no Welsh blood having fun at the expense of those who do.

Andres went into the army a year before me. He was in Class 62 and I was in 63. I didn't know that he was in the Malvinas at all. A little while after I got home I heard that Austin hadn't come back.

How do I feel about the whole business by now? That I was conned! The only thing I would wish is that this will never happen again in that way, not to my sons, not to my brothers, not to anybody. It was such a dreadful experience, and a lot of suffering for nothing.

9. WIL HOWARTH, AMLWCH

There's a big red shiny taxi in front of the house in Llanfairfechan, with the name *Wil Go Cabs* on its side. It's a sunny Sunday afternoon on the only day of the week when Wil Howarth isn't behind the wheel. But if the taxi is idle, its owner isn't – he's busy mixing cement for his paths in the back garden. He can't keep still for a minute, he says. After soldiering for over twenty years he hates being idle and mulling over his thoughts.

Wil Howarth left the Army in the summer of 2002. By then he was a Sergeant working in the recruiting office in Bangor. At the end of that period he attended a course on running his own business. The result was *Wil Go Cabs*. I got to know him in 2002, while preparing a programme for the *Byd ar Bedwar* team, marking the twentieth anniversary of the Falklands war.

A year later I was there again meeting him in Llanfairfechan. After Wil had used up all the cement on his paths, we were back in the same pub as the previous year, with me asking the same questions about the same experiences. Wil preferred to stand by the bar rather than sit still. But once again he told his story in a matter–of-fact way, without emotion and with a fair bit of humour. You need some of that after having been through hell on the *Sir Galahad*.

I was brought up in Amlwch Port on Anglesey. I left school earlier than you were supposed to and everything went down hill after that. Working at first for the Council, making footpaths and such. I didn't see much future there so I went to work with a plastics company in Amlwch. But the hours and the wages were miserable and one of the lads said, 'Why don't we go down to Pembrokeshire to work in the refineries?' 'Fine,' I said, and down there we went, eight of us altogether. The money was good, about two or three hundred pounds a week, and that was in 1979. The boys at Wimpeys and McAlpines were going on strike for the smallest thing. Because the money was so good they could be on strike and still afford to go on the pop. I started thinking after that about what I wanted to do with my life, and decided to hitch hike to Swansea to the army careers office.

When we had to take the oath of loyalty to the Queen, I said that I wanted it in Welsh. And I got to go into the Welsh Guards at 21. It wasn't easy at first - it was hell of a rough place, with a lot of bullying going on.

By joining the Army Wil Howarth was following a family tradition. His father and his great uncle were both awarded military decorations.

Most of the officers had been to Eton, Harrow, Oxford and Cambridge, places like that. One of them asked me one day who the two men were in the photos I had up on my locker. 'That's my gran's brother,' I said. 'He got the VC, DSO and Bar and the Medal Militaire in the first world war. The one below him is my father. He got an MM and Mentioned in Despatches for escaping from a

Japanese camp in the second world war.' 'By tomorrow,' this officer said, 'I want you to find out who my grandfather was.' So I turned round and said to him 'If you don't know, how the hell am I supposed to find out?' I got into a bit of trouble over that.

In February 1981 Wil joined the Regiment. At the end of that year he spent four months in Kenya. Early on in the following year the talk started about trouble brewing in somewhere called the Falkland Islands. Wil and his crew were sent to Brecon to prepare for war. They trained hard, with other regiments, in the Brecon Beacons, but before going to the Falklands they had to go to Carmarthen to be granted the freedom of the town.

You never saw such a miserable bunch of lads in your life. We didn't want to go to war even though that's what we were trained for, but if we had to go, none of us wanted to be marching here with some councillor taking the salute as we went past.

At the end of training we all went to Southampton and onto the QE2, a huge ship. Who came on board with us but Erika Roe, who had recently been in the news for streaking at that rugby match in Twickenham. The boys were hoping she'd bring her secret weapons all the way to the Falklands with us!

I saw two boys I knew on the QE2. Freddie we called one, because he looked like Freddie Starr. The other was a boy from Amlwch, we called JP. Both of them worked on the ship. That was a good thing because we were all on the 'two can rule' - only supposed to have two small cans of beer a day. Because I knew these two members of the crew, they looked after me.

Even though they'd changed the ship around a bit, like turning the swimming pool deck into a place for helicopters to land, most of her was exactly as it was before, when she was taking people on cruises. The shops were open and the boys had seen all these cameras and lighters, and all sorts of stuff was being pinched! The food at the beginning was the same as they'd have on a cruise. But we'd eaten everything in the kitchen within a week and then we were back on sausage and chips.

About a fortnight after we set off, one of the turbines broke down, and we had to stop. Nobody was happy with this – soldiers hate being on a ship, they're trained for being on land. There were rumours we'd have to turn back. But they managed to repair the ship, and off we went again, crossing the equator. We stopped at Freetown, Sierra Leone, where it was boiling hot. The QE2 is about three or four stories high and the lads were throwing tomatoes down to the children, who caught them, thinking they were oranges. There were all kinds of tricks like that being played.

After that the weather changed, and changed again. We were transferred from the QE2 to the *Canberra*, an old ship - rusty and looking like she'd fall apart. In Grytviken, South Georgia, we saw a shot-down helicopter, a wrecked submarine on the quay and a holed corvette. I remember thinking at the time, 'That's it now, the shit has kicked off'.

Towards the end of the journey the soldiers were transferred from the *Canberra* to a tug called *Typhoon*. Wil Howarth and his crew landed in San Carlos Bay on East Falkland and were ordered to move to a place called Bomb Alley, which didn't sound too promising.

At least we were on land, and feeling safe. We were soldiers, not sailors. The first thing we had to do was dig trenches in the wet ground – so we could live in them. As soon as we dug them they would fill up with water. We were there for two days and one night, before starting to move on again. The Paras were already moving ahead towards Goose Green and Darwin, and we had to go around another way. The idea was that we would march through the night to Bluff Cove, near Stanley. The ground was wet and hellish to walk through, full of what we used to call 'babies' heads'. These were round tufts and when you stood on them with a heavy weight on your back your leg would give way. That happened to a lot of the boys. We were carrying between 10 and 13 stone on our backs, and trying to climb the slopes on those mountains even with nothing on your back would have been enough of a job. Each time one of the lads fell, it took two others to look after him. Many of us were suffering from trench foot, something I thought belonged in the first world war. In the end they decided that we couldn't walk any further, it was too dangerous.

It was fine for the Paras - what they did was drop their heavy gear, which was picked up by the choppers, and then move on. But we had to carry everything ourselves - there were no choppers to be had. After the war Max Hastings wrote a book where he says that the boys of the Welsh Guards weren't as fit as the Paras. But in the previous year we had beaten the whole Army in the rugby, we had defeated the Paras in the *Super Platoon* in Berlin and beaten everybody at athletics. And that turnip-head dared to say we weren't fit!

But they decided we should turn back, and that they would take us around by ship. About that time we saw some SAS lads, or the 'Hereford Hooligans' as we called them - wherever they go something gets destroyed. They had just 'done' Pebble Island. They wore baseball caps, and us with all the gear! They didn't care, they just did their own thing.

Next we were on our way by sea, on the *Sir Galahad*, from San Carlos to what's now known as Bluff Cove or Port Fitzroy - although its real name is Port Pleasant. *HMS Glasgow* was with us giving cover, a solid old ship even though there was already a hole in her side where a bomb had gone through her. All night when we arrived there Platoon Company, the Anti-Tanks and others were busy being unloaded - but for some reason, half way through, everything stopped, nothing was moving, and the boys were starting to worry.

Next day I went up on deck for a smoke and to look around. There was a mountain nearby, and if you can see the mountain, the mountain can see you. If there were any FACs – Forward Air Controllers - that's where their observation post would be, where they would be best placed to observe and bring in the planes. Then I looked for *HMS Glasgow* and she wasn't there. She had a modern air defence system, but she had gone. And I knew that the *Galahad* was an old ship. Her guns were old-fashioned and all worked off the engine - if the engine was destroyed, the guns wouldn't work.

It was a fine day and the sun was shining - you can get all four seasons in one day in these places. With me was one of my friends, Mark Eames from Bangor. Mark has a stammer. Here he was looking at me and me looking at him. 'F-f-fucking sitting ducks,' he said, and nothing could have been more true. We were like a duck, sitting right there on the water.

In the meantime the soldiers overheard a fierce argument between two officers about what should be done next: to move the men off the ship, or move the equipment. According to Wil the argument raged for three to four hours without a decision being reached. In the end one officer said to the other that he would be to blame if anything were to happen to the boys.

Around three or four o'clock in the afternoon we hear 'Air Raid Warning Red'- the highest level alert. That one was a false alarm. I went down to the other deck and this screaming started again, with the Mirages and the Skyhawks and all sorts coming overhead. And the next thing was the ship had caught it in the stern. We were unloading pallets of ammunition at the time and a bomb hit right in the middle of all that, with rounds of bullets and all sorts going off like psychedelic fireworks. There was a forklift in front of me and that hit me in the chest, knocked me out. When I came to, it was like being inside a tin of beans that was being squeezed. Then I heard the voice of my friend Mark Eames shouting 'W-w-w-Wil...' The bang had made his stammer worse, but he was trying to tell me that some lad had broken his leg or something. One minute it was light, the next it was dark, and I couldn't see them. I was worried about the Engineers who were with us, because they were carrying explosives and sleeping beside them to keep them stable. If they went off behind us, then that would be the end of it. But thank God, they had all managed to escape from the ship. At last I found Mark and this boy named Steve Brennan. He hadn't broken his leg but he was in shock, so I said to Mark 'Put him on your shoulder and take him out.' By now Mark had gone and I was on my knees on the floor searching for people. I didn't know if there was anyone, living or dead, around me. But after Mark had gone someone closed the door as they left and then I couldn't get out. I thought the end had come. But luckily someone opened it again, and up I went.

There was a terrible mess on the deck. I wasn't feeling any pain. Everything was surreal. Like in slow-motion. Arms and legs all over the place. Bodies burning. It was so hot that the ship was turning red and buckling like waves. Some of the boys were jumping over the side trying to get into the boats, most of them with burns, going into water that was minus five or minus ten. If the burns didn't kill them they would have hypothermia within a couple of minutes. And then the choppers came in trying to blow the boats away from the back end of the ship with their blades. The pilots of these choppers were hellishly brave.

I saw Simon Weston being lifted from the deck in only his underpants, in so much pain that he shouted 'Somebody shoot me!' about three times. I pull his leg now and say if he'd shouted once more, I would have done it!

I was helping some of the lads who'd been hurt, giving some of them morphine or whatever, and putting a number on their foreheads to say when they'd had it. Then the choppers came for the rest of us. Everyone was pretty calm to tell the truth. 'It's your turn next, and then yours...' Me and the skipper, Captain Roberts, and the medic Steve Jones were the last three to leave the ship. They told me to jump when the chopper was on its way up. That's when I felt my leg click. The cartilage had come out.

We went down next to Bluff Cove and there was a

sheep shed there, which is where they kept us. Another air raid warning came and they told us to go out into the trench. I'd gone into delayed shock by now, and was refusing to talk to anyone. It was then, I think, that my personality changed. Everyone was in shock, with people being moved around everywhere. They put me on another ship, the *Fearless*. Somebody had opened the bar there and I got my hands on two cans of beer. 'Hey, I thought you were dead,' said the Company Commander to me. 'Sorry to disappoint you,' I said.

Then we went ashore and to a bunker in Ajax Bay. Some of the lads were wounded and we moved in to get new kit and stuff like that. That's where we saw Commander Jolly who became famous for looking after the Argies. Some prisoners were there in the lock-up, with the Red Cross there making sure they weren't mistreated. They got better food and care than we did. It was there that I saw some of them listening to us speaking Welsh, and one or two of them asked us for tea and other things in Welsh. I'm sure that some of them understood what we were saying, but I don't think any of them could speak Welsh properly.

After only another four or five days there was the ceasefire and we all went to Port Stanley to clear up and look after the POWs. Then we got sent to the airport to get rid of the ice on the runway. Because the Harriers burned so much fuel during vertical take-off, they wanted them to use the runway in the normal way. But one of them started to wobble, then another, and what Harriers do automatically if they're going to crash is to get rid of all ammunition. That's what happened and a Sidewinder missile went into the middle of seven or eight of the boys. Nobody was killed, but almost all of them lost an arm or a leg. This was all kept quiet at the time, as if nothing had happened, but we knew that it had.

Now that it was over, the boys from the *Galahad* and those who had been ashore didn't always see eye to eye. One would say to the other, 'I'd rather be on the ship than on land.' And we would say: 'Don't be so stupid, you had a chance to do something and you did it.' They were on a guilt trip. It took a couple of years before the lads all bonded as a group again.

We left Port Stanley and I looked for the ship that would take us home but there was nothing there. All I could see was a cross-channel ferry called the *St. Edmund*. So we had to travel from the South Atlantic to Ascension Island on that flat-bottomed boat! She was all over the place. And what did they do but stick us and one of the Para squadrons there together. That was a big mistake, especially after the bar opened. Every night was the same, we'd have a pint and then there would be a fight.

We unloaded in Ascension, and flew from there to Brize Norton. Who was there to meet us, but Carlo?* He shook hands with all of us. One of the lads said to him, 'I didn't know you were with us, never saw you on the plane coming back.' The boys had no patience with that sort of thing. All we wanted to do was go home and get on with our lives.

All our kit and documents went down on the *Galahad*. About a month later, after we got home, we still hadn't received any pay. 'Your documents aren't here, so we can't pay you,' they said. Not a penny. My first wife and I had a daughter one or two years old at the time. How was I supposed to feed them and myself with no money?

---

* The Prince of Wales, see Glossary

When I got back to the battalion afterwards everyone stood at parade and suddenly there was a loud 'Wooow!', like a low-flying plane. I don't know what it was, a hoax or something, but half the boys hit the deck. And this bloke said: 'Stand up! What's the matter with you?' But he hadn't been there, had he?

Everything was changing now and they wanted to be rid of the boys who'd been in the Falklands. Some had burns and some had lost arms and legs, so they had to get shot of them. There was a new crowd coming in, and they didn't like the lads who'd been in the Falklands, so it was a hell of a job carrying on after that. They saw me as a sort of loose cannon, a dangerous creature. I wasn't of course. As long as people kept their distance and left me alone, then I had a pretty good life.

Wil was glad of the chance to spend a week back in the Falklands in 2002, in very different circumstances from his earlier time there, in the company of his friend Howard 'Josk' Jones and a television crew.

I wanted to lay the ghost to rest, as they say. People said that I was too angry, too ready to get in a fight and I thought it would do me good to go back. So when the chance came, I decided to go. The journey down was good. We stopped at Santiago and other places. But I wasn't prepared for the visit to the islands. That was like going back to a graveyard. Nothing had changed about the place. I even found the hole in the ground where I had lived. And the sheep shed where I went into shock.

What effect did the war have on me? It makes you hard as hell to live with for the people around you. I haven't got much much patience with fools. Anything that needs doing, I do it straight away or don't bother at all. I've got no patience with anyone who complains all the time, 'I've got to do this, or I've got to do that'. I say to them, 'Shut up, get on and do it.' There are a lot of people who think I'm not like them, and they're right. After twenty years in the army you're not the same as people who haven't been there. When I meet people like Josk we get on fine with each other, but those around us don't always get on with us. I wasn't angry before I went in but yes, the army changed me. Not just in the Falklands. I did three years in Ireland afterwards. That, by itself, without going to war, changes someone. You don't know who's your friend and who's the enemy, so you don't trust anyone. That's the same with me and Josk, we trust no one, only each other. You're used to working in teams of four, and you trust only those four. It's a hell of a thing, because it's a clique, but it's a clique that works and you know you can trust the other lad with your life.

Some of the other boys have suffered more than me. Everybody's different. There's a label on it now, Post Traumatic Stress Disorder, and there's a place in Llandudno, Tŷ Gwyn, where some of the lads go to get treatment. They can't handle life outside but they feel safe there because they're with people the same as them. You're like a ticking time-bomb. You're braced for anything. You look closely at everyone who comes into the pub, sitting with your back to the wall most often. You know you're safe there. With me, I have to be doing something all the time. I'm only still when I'm asleep. If I sit down and start thinking, the whole thing comes back.

Wil Howarth has an interest in Patagonia and would like to go there some day. He asked me a question I couldn't answer: what sort of welcome could someone expect after having fought against the Argentinian army? But did Wil himself realise, during the war, that there could have been Welshmen on the other side?

They told us on the ship on the way out that it was a possibility. And I remembered being taught when I was at school about Patagonia, about them leaving from Anglesey and other places after being lumbered with the English and all that. It was strange to be thinking on the way out, what if you were to meet some of these people, and them speaking the same language as you? Maybe you'd kill a relative of yours, you wouldn't know. But the thing is, when someone's in a war you can't afford to let any weakness into your head, you've got no choice but to carry on. If you're a jockey in the Grand National you have to strike, to win. There are no 'ifs, buts or maybes', you have to carry on.

In any war, if you give a boy of fourteen a gun, he just has to pull the trigger. It doesn't matter who the enemy is. You're not going to stop and think of his age or who he is before shooting him. You don't think about it because if you did it would be you who'd be catching it. 'Ours not to reason why, just to do and die.' You can't afford to have a conscience when you go to war.

10. HORACIO JOSE KENT, TRELEW

You might not think it at first but Horacio Kent has borne more than his share of life's burdens. He lost his father when he was three years old, and recently lost his wife - leaving him to care for a son and daughter, now aged nine and three, whose photographs sit on a shelf behind his desk. Between the two tragedies he spent 74 days living in a wet hole in the ground on an island in the Malvinas, expecting to be bombed and watching his friends die. He told me that he has talked little of this experience in the past twenty years, but he was glad of the opportunity to do so now in 2002 - because there were things that needed to be said. So I landed, with Luned Gonzalez again translating, at his office near Trelew town centre where he runs a car insurance company.

It was a shame that we needed a translator at all. You don't have to dig deep to discover Horacio Kent's rudiments of the Welsh language. He can say 'Sudach chi', 'bara menyn', 'teisen blât', and other phrases which form part of the social fabric of Y Wladfa's Welsh. Perhaps, then, he could have been one of the Argentinians the soldiers from Wales claimed they had heard speaking the occasional sentence in Welsh in the course of the Malvinas war? No, definitely not, he said. He had not realised at the time that there were Welsh soldiers fighting against him. He believed all the enemy to be English. The only ones he recognised as not English were the Gurkhas – about whom there were stories of atrocities carried out in the course of the conflict.

Horacio Kent doesn't need much questioning or prompting. He tells his story without fuss or self-pity.

I was born and raised on my grandfather and grandmother's farm in Dolavon. The name Kent came from England. My great grandfather went originally to North America, and from there to Argentina. My grandmother was a Brunt and she was originally from Wales. She and my grandfather spoke Welsh all the time. But there was no Welsh on my mother's side, where the forefathers were Spanish. My father was one of eight children. I spoke Welsh myself as a child, especially with my Auntie Gwen. After she died there were few opportunities to speak the language and I have forgotten most of it.

I had just finished secondary school when the war began. I was 19 years old and had started my military service in the Army on the twelfth of February. On the fourth of April I was in the Malvinas. So I'd been a soldier for less than three months, with very little training. I had been in Comodoro Rivadavia, in the Regimento 8 de Infanterio - Eighth Infantry Regiment.

We didn't know at the time about any conflict brewing in the Malvinas. They told us that we were to be sent to Tucuman, a state in North West Argentina, to deal with some guerrilla fighters. It was the second of April and we were training hard when the call came for the regiment to assemble on the square, the Plaza de Armas, at seven o'clock in the morning. We sang the Argentinian national anthem and then we were told that Argentina had won back the Malvinas Islands.

The following day they issued us with full military uniform, a rifle each from the 1940s and a rucksack with some essentials. Then they put us on a Fokker aircraft and we were in Puerto Argentino on the Malvinas by six o'clock on the morning of the fourth of April.

The first impression was of a beautiful place. The fields were so green in the Malvinas. The bushes grew tall but the grass was cropped short, almost like a golf course. There wasn't much of a connection between us and the islanders. What little contact there was suggested that, quite reasonably, they weren't too happy to see us. I was in Puerto Argentino for fifteen days and then I was moved to another island, Gran Malvina (West Falkland). We stayed there at a place named Bahia Zorro, or Fox Bay as we called it.

From then on we were on the front line of battle. We hid in holes in the ground, but every time there was an attack we were the first to catch it. They attacked us from the air and from ships, but there was no ground assault because they weren't keen to land where we were. That was because of a strategy we had developed to trick them. Along the coast we positioned rows of metal pipes as a decoy. On their radar these looked like anti-aircraft guns, but none of us were anywhere near that area during their attacks.

There was always about ten centimetres of water in the holes we were living in. Then winter came and it started to snow. The holes were just about a metre and a quarter by a metre and a half in size, and a little over half a metre in depth. The ground was saturated and the holes would often fill up. We would then raise the floor higher with stones. I lived like that for 74 days without washing once. I was still in the same clothes and they were starting to rot on me. My long-johns had stretched and kept falling down.

Life was very tough and things got even harder after the English closed down the straits between the two main islands. We got our food from Puerto Argentino, everything had to arrive there. But by now anything attempting to land was being shot down, so there was no food reaching us. The threat of starvation was the biggest problem, but not the only one. The water in our boots and socks meant that everyone's feet suffered very badly. Even though we were bombed every now and then, it was more of a battle against our own conditions and against the elements than anything else, a war to stay alive from day to day.

At the weekends, at night, they used to attack us from the air. Some of the English told us afterwards that the reason for that was the double-time pay they received at night, but I don't know if that was true. We never fired back at the planes, or they would have found our positions and dropped everything they had on our heads. Not many of us got killed by the bombs because they didn't know where to aim them.

We heard nothing about the progress of the war. The only news we got was that we were winning, and killing many of the English, but of course that was all lies.

But one night we received orders to surrender, because the war had come to an end. We were in our positions and they told us on the radio to go to sheds at the estancia, or large farm, about four kilometres to our rear. The commanding officer of the regiment, Senior Captain Garzon, told us that Menendez had already surrendered, and that we must lay down our arms. We were to destroy all the weapons and motorised vehicles we had before the English came, so there would be nothing left they could use. And that's what we did. Two days later the English arrived.

The only food to be had was what we had sent to the people living on the estancia. And sheep, that's what saved my life. I was used to killing and roasting sheep at home in Patagonia, and not many of the other soldiers had ever done that before. Towards the end the sheep also were becoming scarce, and we searched for mussels on the beach. There was one lad from Cordoba, Argentina's second city, who died of botulism because he ate food that had gone bad, food we had thrown away. Many other soldiers died the same way.

The English arrived by landing craft after dark. They treated us very well. They collected personal details from us all, then we were put on helicopters and flown out to sea. We had no idea what was happening to us, but we were ordered to jump from the helicopter into a landing craft, and then that ferried us to a ship, the *Norland*, which was to take us back to Puerto Madryn. All this happened in the middle of the night.

The ship was packed with troops, Argentinian and English. They asked us if anyone spoke English. I spoke a little having been taught by Eirie John Lloyd and Eileen de Jones at William Morris School in Dolavon. So I was taken on as translator , distributing food, toilet paper and so on as well as spending a lot of time in the kitchen with the British soldiers. I slept in a cabin, sharing with two others, with a comfortable bed, hot water and a bath - perfection!

It was good being able to communicate with the British soldiers. That's when you realised the difference between them and our soldiers. We had no chance against them in a war, not under any circumstances. What happened to our Argentinian lads was a massacre.

The English soldiers treated me very well now that the

war was over. It's difficult to describe the near starvation we had suffered. They fed me well and because I was distributing food to the others I could stay in the kitchen which meant I ate twice as much food as the rest of them! During the four days it took us to reach Puerto Madryn, food was rationed, everyone being allowed one cheese and ham sandwich, two boiled eggs and a half litre of milk at each meal.

It was interesting on board to observe the behaviour of our senior military officers - the higher echelons of the Argentinian army. As they got to the ship many of them had ripped their stripes off. They wanted to give the impression that they were ordinary soldiers - to dodge any problems with the British. In our view, as ordinary Argentinian soldiers, this was cowardice. We regarded them as being like villains in a film. When it came time for them to face up to their responsibilities, they weren't prepared to do so.

We came into Puerto Madryn at eleven o'clock one morning. The whole population was there waiting for us. The *Canberra* had arrived before us. I was moved from there to an air base in Trelew, and welcomed by a relative who was in the Army. He gave me food and told my mother in Dolavon where I was. The family wasn't allowed to see me. We were in a bad state through malnutrition and the authorities didn't want us to be seen like that. Then the whole regiment was taken by bus to Comodoro Rivadavia. I stayed there for a further six weeks, recovering and getting plenty of food. I wasn't receiving any medical treatment. But many of the other lads with me in the war were and some are still in poor health even today.

I haven't suffered any problems, mental or physical,

thank God. I was always strong. After the war I felt no bitterness towards anyone. I just set about working and forgetting about what had happened. I don't usually go to ex-servicemen's centres though I'll help if anyone ever asks me for anything. I don't dig into the past from day to day

I still believe for many reasons that Argentina owns the Malvinas. But I have to say that the British who live there have looked after the place better than we would have. I'm in favour of some sort of integration, with freedom for them to come here and for us to go there. Their traditions, naturally, are very different from ours, and we went there to interfere in their business after a century and a half of them having been there.

One thing still troubles me after the war. There is a cemetery in Puerto Argentino where most of the Argentinian soldiers who died are buried. Where I was, on the other island, seventeen, eighteen, possibly twenty of our crew were killed. Some of them were close friends of mine. The one who died of botulism by my side in a hole in the ground is there. Another from Cordoba was killed by a bomb exploding. I'm sure their remains are still in the same place – neither the British nor anyone else would have bothered to move them. I woud like to return to the islands once again to pay my respects to them, and to make sure that they are buried with everyone else in the cemetery at Puerto Argentino.

11. ARTHUR WYN WILLIAMS, MORFA NEFYN

The *QE2* had long since crossed the equator, and the weather became colder as she sped south. The baggage master, Selwyn Jones, suddenly heard his name on the tannoy. Within minutes he was knocking on the door of cabin 2010. This was opened by his brother-in-law Arthur Wyn Williams. In the circumstances, Selwyn's question seemed sensible enough: 'What the hell are you doing here?' No one had told him that Arthur, his sister's husband, had received last minute orders to join the task force on its way to the Falklands. 'Our legs felt like jelly,' says Arthur today. 'It was hard to tell which one of us would be the first to collapse'.

Today, Selwyn has retired from the sea and lives in Efail Newydd on the Llŷn Peninsula, while Arthur manages a home for the elderly in Pwllheli. The two often meet, to plant potatoes or tidy up their gardens, sometimes to play pool. Memories of that voyage to the South Atlantic are still vivid for them both, the soldier still thankful to the sailor for the occasional favours he received.

'When I had a spare moment I'd nip down to the galley and have a little drink with the crew,' says Arthur. 'I wasn't supposed to go, but Selwyn would smuggle me down there in the food lift.'

Arthur, the son of a sailor who later became a coastguard in Porthdinllaen, had been in the army for over twelve years before being called to the Falklands.

I started with MANWEB as an apprentice electrician at first, but to be honest I was a naughty boy there and got sacked. I started work then with a company from London here in Llŷn, but they went bust. I went to Bangor, thinking of joining the RAF, but when I got there it happened that the man had gone for lunch. So I crossed the corridor and spoke to the Army man. That's how I ended up there. That was a big disappointment for my father, who expected me to go to sea like he did.

I went into the Royal Corps of Signals to be a linesman, as they were known in the old days - telecommunications mechanics is what they're called now. Because of my experience with MANWEB I could put telephone lines up on the poles and so on. And off I went aged seventeen to Catterick in Yorkshire to do the training. I was posted then, in 1970, to the Seventh Armoured Brigade, or the Desert Rats, at a place near Hamburg.

After a subsequent stint in Oman, Arthur came home and got married to Carys, before moving again to an airfield on the Dutch-German border. Their son, Ian, was born and at nine months old became severely ill with a brain tumour. Ian was treated at Great Ormond Street Hospital , London, and then at Clatterbridge in Cheshire.

While Ian was in Clatterbridge I got posted to Liverpool with the Territorials so we could be close to each other as a family. But after a year there the Army told me I had to make my mind up about what I was going to do. Ian's treatment had left him blind and the Army had no facilities at all to help us look after him. So I had to choose between the Army and my boy. We spent a month or more pondering this and talking to the doctors. They didn't think little Ian had much time left to live. We found a place for him in a Sunshine Home for the blind in Southport, which was run by nuns.

Arthur and his wife Carys went back to Germany, where Arthur was promoted to Sergeant. He was then posted back to HQ in Aldershot

I'd only been back two days when I got a message that I had 24 hours to pack my bags and head for the Falklands. 'I've only just got home,' I said, so they gave me ten days to visit my son and organize everything with my wife at this end.

Most of the task force had sailed from Southampton and Portsmouth, with all the flags and the cameras, by the time Arthur took a flight to Ascension Island, where he boarded *HMS Cardiff* to meet up with his fellow soldiers, and his brother-in-law, on the QE2.

The rest of my group had been together for some time, and here was I suddenly landing in the middle of them. It wasn't the best of starts but we got over that in the following week. My Squadron Commander briefed me and told me exactly what I was supposed to do. He was called Major Forge, a bit of a cowboy, wearing a Colt 45 with ivory grips.

We trained on the QE2 on the way down: running

three laps around the ship with the Gurkhas, starting at four o'clock in the morning. Then the ship's crew would load heaps of rubbish into black bags and throw them in the sea so we could practice shooting at them. I learned later that there was a submarine with us under the ship for the whole journey, especially as we neared South Georgia, in case they tried to sink us. There would have been dreadful trouble if Maggie had lost the QE2.

The work of the Royal Signals in the Falklands was to set up and maintain telephone networks enabling the different sections of the military to communicate with each other. Arthur reached Goose Green the day after Colonel H Jones and scores of others on both sides were killed there. While the Royal Signals established their headquarters in Goose Green, the infantry was still pushing forward towards Port Stanley.

The radio equipment we had didn't work in gullies, so we needed to set up relay stations on hilltops. We had sent out four lads to arrange this with enough water and rations for two or three days, and the end of the third day was approaching. Major Forge and the Staff Sergeant, Joe Baker, had got hold of a Gazelle helicopter to go looking for them. Joe Baker was a friend of mine. We'd had a few pints together on the QE2 on the way down. Major Forge was the 'cowboy' I mentioned before. 'I'll go and sort it out,' he said. It was a quiet, clear, moonlit night and we heard the sound of the Gazelle leaving. Around midnight there was a bang, and we thought someone had started bombing. But at about half-past three the news came through. Someone had forgotten to tell the Navy that the helicopter was on its way, and they had picked her up on the radar and thought she was one of the enemy's. It was *HMS Cardiff* that brought the Gazelle down. Joe Baker, Major Forge and the three crew members were killed instantly.

Within another couple of days Arthur witnessed the biggest catastrophe to hit his fellow Welshmen during the course of the war.

We had crossed from Goose Green to Fitzroy on a small ship, a coaster used to carry lambs and food between the islands and Argentina. Then we had established our headquarters in this big hangar, although many of us thought that was a mistake - one bomb and we'd all have copped it. *HMS Tristram* and *HMS Galahad* had arrived there the previous night. Next day I was on duty, making sure the telephones were working properly, when there was a hell of an explosion. It felt as if all the air was being sucked out of the shed, and everybody ran outside.

There was a major panic. I went back in the hangar, grabbed a telephone and a pack of D10 - half a mile of cable. I tied one end to a post, ran down to where the ships were on fire and set up a link between HQ and the bridgehead commander. By this time some helicopters had arrived and were trying to blow the lifeboats away from the ships with their downwash. There were huge explosions and a smell of burning, black smoke, and these lads being carried to shore on the boats, skin peeling away in curls off the fingers and hands of some of them, faces burnt black. In my whole life I've seen nothing like it. After another twelve hours, it was all finished, the place completely quiet. I didn't know any of the lads on the *Galahad*. It was very sad thinking they were Welsh boys...

Before the white flag was raised over Port Stanley news reached Arthur which, at that moment, made the war seem almost irrelevant.

The RSM came to see me, and I could see from his face that something big had gone wrong. 'Here we go,' I said to myself, 'I'm being shifted somewhere else again.' He took me aside and said 'Let's go for a walk.' I realised he wanted to tell me something, but what exactly I didn't know. He had news from home, a telegram saying that little Ian had passed away. He had got meningitis in the care home in Southport. He was eight and a half years old and had been fighting for his life since the age of one. I remembered the words of the doctor in Clatterbridge, when Ian was just nine months old, that they reckoned he had only three to six months more to live. The last time I saw him before leaving for the Falklands one of the staff told me that he still liked ice cream for pudding, and that he had learned to swim. That's what first came to my mind. The poor RSM was crying but at that moment I couldn't, I was so much in shock.

* * *

In 1986, by now a Sergeant Major, Arthur had the opportunity to return to the Falklands for nine months. On Remembrance Sunday he was at a service to commemorate his friends killed in the helicopter. He says that period, four years after the war, helped him come to terms with his earlier experiences.

Half way through that tour I got a few days off, and chose to spend them on a tiny place called Penguin Island.

There were a couple of huts there left for people who liked to take penguin photographs. That first night I slept like a pig, I was so tired. Next day, I went to take some pictures and it took me hours to realise that the penguins were happy to come towards me if I bent down below their height. If I lay on my stomach they came quite close, but every time I got to my feet they ran away. I was on my own in the silence, with only the sound of the sea breeze.

By the second night, it was as if I was wide awake again after being in some kind of half dream since 1982. That's when I realised exactly what had happened to me, where I had been, what I had seen, losing my mates, what I had seen on the *Tristram* and *Galahad*, and especially losing little Ian. Till then I had locked all of it away somewhere in the back of my head. I was awake all night, thinking, smoking and drinking tea. When I got up the next morning, a huge weight was off my shoulders. From that weekend on I have been able to shake it all out of my mind and get on with my life.

12. JULIO OSCAR GIBBON, ESQUEL

Esquel in Cwm Hyfryd is a town built to a grid plan on level ground at the bottom of a bowl created by the surrounding mountains. In one of the grid's squares, enclosed by a high fence, is the headquarters of the Gendarmeria, the Border Guards. The Argentinian border with Chile is not far away. I was on my way to the HQ to interview one of the guards there. After getting used to meeting ex-conscripts, who had been sent to the Malvinas raw and untrained and against their will, I was looking forward to interviewing one who had gone there by choice. Julio Oscar Gibbon was a soldier before there was any mention of the war, and he remains one to this day.

I was not sure what kind of welcome to expect at a military camp being a British citizen, whether Welsh or otherwise. But at least I had with me a guide and translator with the best possible credentials. Aira Hughes and her husband Elgar live within a block or two of the headquarters - though it would have been easy to forget, from their warm Welsh welcome, that I was even in an Argentinian town. I could just as easily have been sitting at a hearth in the country in Dyffryn Clwyd, or Montgomeryshire. Aira used to be a teacher at the local primary school in Esquel and Julio Oscar Gibbon had been one of her pupils. Better yet, her father had served in the Gendarmeria.

The surname Gibbon is famous for many reasons among the Welsh families of Y Wladfa. The first of the family arrived in Patagonia from Loughor, near Swansea, with the early settlers. He had five sons, two of them among the founders and notables of Seion Chapel in Esquel. But another brother followed a totally different path. Mansel Gibbon's nickname was 'the Rebel' and, according to the description of him in R. Bryn Williams's book *Y Wladfa*, it was fully justified. He was a companion of Wilson and Evans, the two bandits who shot dead Llwyd ap Iwan in Nant y Pysgod in 1909, one of the most shocking incidents in Y Waldfa's history. Mansel Gibbon himself spent most of his life on the run. A local policeman believed he had shot him during an attempted escape across a river, but the Rebel had swum to safety under water. He later went to Chile, married a German girl, and lived a comfortable life.

Julio Oscar Gibbon is the great grandson of one of the Rebel's more respectable brothers. Apart from the fact that he too wore a pistol at his hip, there was nothing threatening or wild about him as he welcomed us to the headquarters of the Gendarmeria. He was very happy to see his old teacher, and to all appearances, quite prepared to welcome me to his office as well.

I had anticipated a problem with taking his photograph. The tourist books warned that it was unwise to carry a camera close to military installations in Argentina. When we were led into an empty room to hold our interview, my hope was to perhaps take his photograph there. 'Si, si,' he said when Aira asked him, then suggested it might be better to take a picture outside. So off we went to the drill square, enclosed on all sides by buildings and named after one of his fellow-soldiers who did not return from the Malvinas. It was a Saturday afternoon, and there was hardly anyone else around the camp, but as we prepared to take the photo a tall, upright, authoritative figure approached us. He was introduced to me as the camp's commanding officer. He had come there to greet us and wish us well.

Back in the office, Julio answered all our questions instantly, you could almost say like a shot from a gun. It was clear, almost before hearing the translation, that the doubts and concerns agitating some of the other, more discontented, ex-combatants for the last twenty years had never crossed the mind of this professional soldier.

I was working here in the Gendarmeria before the war in the Malvinas, but they also trained us for other types of work. I volunteered, among other things, for a Commando course which prepared us physically and mentally for what we would face in the Malvinas. That was the main purpose of the course.

Then we went to Comodoro Rivadavia and from there in a Hercules to Puerto Argentino. This was in May, when the fighting on the islands had already begun. We arrived there on a Friday. On the Saturday we were examining the terrain, and by Sunday six of our squadron had already lost their lives in the battle. In total, we lost seven from our squadron during the war, with two wounded. I remember their names. Nassif, Pereira, Guerrero, Parada ...

We were based in Puerto Argentino but our job in special forces was to go out on patrol every afternoon into enemy territory. I was at Mount Kent, Mount Two Sisters, all those places. They would bombard us from the air in the mornings and evenings, and from their ships at night. It was a psychological battle more than anything - they were preventing us from sleeping. The bombing and the shooting never stopped.

As special forces soldiers, under the command of Rico and Seineldin, our squadron would go out every day behind enemy lines, sometimes the front line, sometimes into the second and third lines. We were in several battles whose names I can't remember. In spite of all our training, we hadn't expected to see anything like this.

The last three days were horrific. By then the British had penetrated everywhere on the islands. Our front line started to withdraw but the rear rank was still firing at the enemy. It was total chaos, and many of our boys were being killed by our own soldiers.

One night we got caught between the two front lines. The tracer bullets fired from both sides meant the place was lit up like day. We had no choice but to stand up to the enemy and fight. We were better trained than they were in physical combat, but they had far superior back up in the way of helicopters, tanks and planes. They came at us screaming and shouting - all part of the psychological warfare. But many of them fell in that battle.

I didn't sleep at all in the last days of the fighting. Towards the end we were supposed to guard the airfield, but we couldn't deal with it, the British were everywhere. Most of our soldiers were children, terrified, running in all directions. The day before the surrender, I had been wounded and was in Puerto Argentino. That's when the English reached there. The surrender was announced at five past nine in the morning. The English arrived in a small tank and saw the Argentinian Flag and a sign saying 'Aqui no Falklands, Puerto Argentino.' They pulled the flag down and raised the Union Jack in its place.

All the war mementos our squadron brought back are kept in the Centinela, the headquarters of the National Gendarmeria in Buenos Aires. In one battle we walked into an ambush on a bridge. The fighting ranged from one end to the other. We killed four of the enemy and captured their equipment. That's all in the Centinela. We also managed to hold on to the flag of the Escuadron Alacran - the name of our squadron. We carried it throughout the war and didn't want to lose it at the end. So we hid it in the lining of a coat to bring it home. That is kept in Buenos Aires as well

We were held prisoner in Puerto Argentino for three days, then ferried out to the *Canberra* which took us back to Argentina. I was on deck five, one of 347 men in our division. One of the soldiers guarding us, a lance corporal, spoke a little Spanish. He said that it hadn't been worth it, travelling all that way to fight, and that the war hadn't been of any use to us either.

After getting home I went back to the Gendarmeria, went through a full medical, and started work again. I wasn't affected too much by the war because of my training and going there knowing what I was supposed to do. It was different for the boys who were sent into battle with no preparation. I don't think much about the war by now. But as the dates come past each year I still remember everything so clearly. I remember the plane flying us there, just five metres above sea level to avoid the radar - and us having to throw all our kit out while we were still moving. I'm sure the islands will belong to Argentina again one day. I don't know how many years it will take, but it's bound to happen.

'Perhaps he may not want to answer this, still being a soldier,' I said to Aira. 'But would you ask him if he thinks it was worth going there to fight?'

The answer came at once.

Si, si, si. I went there to represent my country, to defend my country and my flag. I went there to offer my life.

On hearing this, his former teacher, smiling and patting him on the back, said: 'Good lad, I taught you that in school!'

13. DENZIL CONNICK,
PONTLLANFRAITH

A small industrial estate in Pontllanfraith. Rows of brown, identical, single-storey units nestled in woodlands that are slowly reclaiming the coalfields of South East Wales. The tenants include light engineering firms, stone masons, an arts studio, an electronics company, a café and, unnoticed in their midst, a unit without so much as a sign - although its work extends across five continents. This is the headquarters of SAMA 82, the creation and workplace of Denzil Connick.

A thick-set man with a moustache, serious yet with a ready smile, Denzil Connick is the secretary of the South Atlantic Medal Association. He was one of the ex-soldiers who founded the society in 1997, in order to safeguard the welfare of those who had been through the war in the South Atlantic fifteen years earlier. No one knows better than Denzil about the sheer agony that war entailed. He reaches for his walking stick as he crosses the office to make a cup of tea. This is the legacy of losing his leg at the end of one of the bloodiest battles of the Falklands on Mount Longdon. I knew about this before but had not realised, until he told me in a matter of fact way in the course of our conversation, that he had 'died' during that attack, before the medics succeeded in restoring his heartbeat.

Denzil Connick is the son of a coal miner who later became a steel-worker. He has deep roots in the area where he lives today, even though he left home at fifteen to join the Army.

I was born in Tredegar. My father was from Merthyr Vale originally and my mother from Cendon near Oakdale. We went to live in Chepstow when I was eight - when my father moved from Oakdale coal mine to Llanwern steelworks. I have three brothers and we were a close-knit family. I left home not because of my family but to look for adventure. I joined the Junior Parachute Company aged fifteen in order to be close to planes. I had always been interested in them, and I was too impatient to wait to join the RAF. I was allowed to join the Parachute Company at an earlier age and believed, rather naively perhaps, that I would find myself working around aircraft.

Aldershot seemed a strange place when I first joined, and I thought I had made a mistake going there. The discipline and routine, I believe, wouldn't have been that different from what would have gone on in a borstal at that time. But I wasn't a young offender - I had volunteered to go there. This was in 1972 and I was starting to wonder what the hell I was doing in these barracks.

I was in the Juniors for two and a half years and then at seventeen I joined the main Regiment. I was in the Third Regiment, and soon got used to life as a young infantryman. I got to see the world - Sudan, Malaya, Singapore, Germany, Denmark, Norway and Italy - before my first tour to Armagh, in Northern Ireland, in 1976. Being sent to Crossmaglen was a pretty frightening experience for a young lad. I lost a close friend there. He was blown up when we were out on patrol. Because you had been well trained, you accepted this kind of thing, which you were taught could happen every now and then. Not that I worried too much about it. To tell the truth I felt more and more enthusiastic about the regiment as the months passed by.

By the time I got to the Falklands in 1982 I was a lance corporal with 3-Para, in the anti-tank platoon. I was working on WOMBAT – 'Weapon of Magnesium Anti-Tank' - and I was the platoon radio operator as well. We sailed there on the *Canberra*, another new experience for me. I was a mature soldier, twenty five years old by then, and many of the young lads with me were only eighteen. The youngest boys in the Paras to die in the Falklands were only seventeen. I was an 'old sweat'. I'd seen the world and made some fantastic friends. The friends you make in the army are true friends, and that makes life easier in difficult times. The other side of the coin is that losing those friends in war can make the grief harder to bear for the survivor.

I was in one of the first waves of troops to land in San Carlos Bay and secure a beachhead on the twenty first of May 1982. In the best tradition of the Parachute Regiment we were out in front, pushing forward to take out as many as we could of the Argentinian soldiers who were closest to us. But we didn't see many. We had to march for seventy miles over rough terrain, almost like being back home in Wales. It was nice seeing everything looking so familiar, and us eight thousand miles from home. For the Paras it was almost like being back on the Brecon Beacons where we did most of our training. It's rough country and it pushes each individual to the limit, making him a better soldier in the end.

The weather was hellish there at the start of a South

Atlantic winter. We knew we were in for a hard time. The Argentinian army had been there long enough to be ready to defend the place. One location they'd be defending was Mount Longdon, outside Stanley. It was one of a number of places, like Tumbledown, Two Sisters and Mount Harriet that we would have to take before we could reach Stanley.

We knew they had a good infantry company on Mount Longdon, with back-up from an equally good marine company. These were not conscripts but professional soldiers. None of us had any experience of the all-out warfare we found ourselves in the middle of now. But we did know that our neighbours in the Welsh Guards had suffered casualties on the *Galahad*, and that our sister battalion, 2-Para, had gone through the battle at Goose Green. We knew very well what was in front of us. It was terrible to think, as we got nearer to the battle at Mount Longdon, that we were bound to lose friends, if not our own lives. That was frightening, but didn't make us any less determined. We knew we had to do the job, and pretty quickly, otherwise we'd lose. And that wasn't part of the 3-Para psyche.

On the evening of July 11th, we were in position to begin the battle of Mount Longdon. 'Fix Bayonets' and here we were facing the enemy. Talk about hell on earth. I'd seen nothing like it in my life. I had trained with live ammunition before then, and had some experience of the noise. But I'd never before encountered the intensity of firing, and that coming straight at us. That was shocking, terrifying in the extreme, rushing towards the trenches and bunkers as we were doing. That's what it was, hand to hand, face to face fighting, with small groups fighting for these positions, many men dying in a very short time over a tiny piece of territory.

It took twelve hours to defeat the enemy on Mount Longdon. I could never describe to you in detail, blow by blow, everything that happened during those twelve hours. There was so much going on, so much courage, there's no way of doing it justice in a conversation like this. To say the least it was a battle terribly hard fought. You have to acknowledge that the enemy fought well. Some of them may have been professionals, but even the conscripts battled hard and we have to give them credit for that. By the end of the fighting 23 of my friends were dead and about 50 were wounded. Many more of the Argentinian boys had been killed and injured. You can imagine it, as dawn broke on the morning of July 13th, the brutality of the battle clear to see on that small piece of land. Bodies everywhere, all over. Men moaning and screaming in pain from their wounds. Witnessing all this, after being embroiled in the battle, was a dreadful experience.

But for Denzil a worse experience, one which changed his whole life, was still to come. The battle of Mount Longdon had been won, but the danger was not over.

We wanted to leave Mount Longdon as quickly as we could and were preparing with our friends from 2-Para to advance to take a place called Wireless Ridge before the final attack on Stanley. Not that I was looking forward to Stanley and the street-fighting – far more get killed in street-fighting that on open ground. There would be severe casualties on both sides, including civilians there. The Argentinian grip on the islands was weakening and I could see the end of the war coming.

But before we could get away from Mount Longdon they were firing at us. Even though they'd lost the battle, their artillery and mortars realised that we were now a target for them. This went on for about two days. That's when I got hit. As it was starting to get dark on July 13th, as we were getting ready to move on to another battle at Wireless Ridge, a shell landed and blew my leg off. My left leg was gone completely, above the knee, just below my hip. And the rest of the leg was a bloody mess. The bones were shattered, shrapnel had gone through my knee, and the femur was sticking out.

I stayed conscious until I reached the field hospital and then I passed out after losing so much blood. They didn't tell me at the time, but I did die in that hospital. They managed to revive me. I became friendly with the anaesthetist afterwards, and he showed me my medical records and how ill I had been. He had to calculate how much anaesthetic he could give me without killing me. One important factor was how much blood I had lost. He told me that he couldn't find a pulse at all, and no blood pressure. So to all intents and purposes I was dead. They had to decide whether they could give me anaesthetic and try to save my life surgically, to stop the bleeding and sort out the terrible mess in the lower half of my body. They must have done the right things or I wouldn't be talking to you now.

I remember coming to on the day after that, the day the war ended. They'd flown me out to the hospital ship *Uganda*. I was still desperately ill, but they told me that the war was over. And that was a relief.

At least I was alive, and I felt that this would be the case at least until I reached home. What worried me most was the thought of dying there, so far from home. And it was a relief to think that no more of my friends would die. Two young boys I was talking to were killed by the bomb that hit me. Before I was wounded I'd carried the bodies of many friends, some of them very close friends indeed. It's a heart-breaking job carrying your friends' bodies. Those are the worst memories I have today of the war. My injuries don't register on the Richter Scale in comparison with memories of my dead friends.

Denzil stayed on the hospital ship sailing around the islands for a month before the doctors decided he was strong enough to fly back to Britain. Then he started another long battle to rebuild his life, physically and mentally.

This was a hard time emotionally, changing from being an exceptionally fit young man, to being a cripple in a wheelchair. But my family was with me, and one good thing happened. One of my very first visitors in hospital was the woman I would marry. Theresa Joyce, as she was then, came originally from Scotland and was a nurse at St Lawrence Hospital, Chepstow, where she worked with my brother. I had known Theresa before going to the Falklands and, to tell the truth, I'd fancied her enormously at that time and, as I later learned, she had fancied me!

She came very soon to see me in hospital, which felt odd at the time, but then she explained why. After hearing about my injuries she was heartbroken and felt that it was important she came.

Afterwards a friend said to me, 'Listen, Theresa has told me how she feels about you, and it's important you take those feelings seriously.' It took a lot of work to convince me. I didn't think any woman in the world would seriously want to be with someone paralysed, as I was. At the time I was full of self-pity. I'd had a shock, but I was still happy that Theresa was taking so much interest. But our relationship developed and we got married on 11th July 1983, a year to the day after the battle on Mount Longdon. I chose that day because I wanted a happy memory to take the place of a terrible memory. It was a good idea at the time, but by now it interferes with our wedding anniversary. When I should be paying attention to Theresa, I'm thinking more about memories of the battle.

I spent most of that first year in hospitals trying to sort out a host of problems, not only physical and emotional, but practical things too. I was on indefinite sick leave, waiting for a discharge from the army on medical grounds. I didn't have to leave. My old CO, Colonel Hew Pike, had said that there would be work to be had in 3-Para for any of his boys, no matter how badly they'd been injured. That appealed to me at first, but as time went by I realised that things would never be the same again. Losing one of your limbs is like losing a close relative. You mourn for your leg as you would for a family member. You go through a period of not being able to believe, afterwards anger, then coming to accept it. I'd come to accept the disability by now, and that's an important part of getting better. Once I'd come to terms with that I could see that the Army couldn't be a choice for me ever again. I'd find it hard to work in the stores or be involved in administration while my mates were doing all the things I used to enjoy. That would do me more harm than good. So in 1984 I left the army, almost a year after we got married.

Soon afterwards Mathew, our first son, arrived, born

in June 1984. His brother Stephen followed in 1986. By now I'd received a very generous grant from the South Atlantic Fund. A grateful British public had set this fund up. The government had nothing to do with it - the government has a lot to answer for in my opinion. As one of the worst injured I got a large sum of money, and the cheque landed on the mat as if I'd won the Pools. And I had no idea what to do with it.

That was a time of sudden change in our lives. Inside a year I had got married, bought a house, my wife was expecting and I had left the army, although still a member of it on paper. I missed my friends even though some of them often came to see me. Hardly a week-end went by in the first six months, maybe a year, without our house being full of friends from the battalion. Theresa enjoyed their company almost as much as I did, delighted with the stories we were telling each other. And this was important for me, part of the process of getting better. It was only with close friends who had been through the same thing that you could talk openly about your experiences. It was like letting off steam - think of a pressure cooker, if you keep the pressure up all the time something's going to blow. Chatting with my mates was like a safety valve, releasing a little bit of steam at a time.

I had to start earning a living, and I decided to go for something self-employed, but doing what I had no idea. I was also beginning to get too fond of the bottle. I started up two businesses, first a small franchise, then a garage business repairing cars that had been in accidents. Both businesses failed within the first year and I lost a lot of money. There were reasons why they failed, and I couldn't blame anybody but myself. I was too naïve, too ready to trust people without realising there were sharks everywhere. Because of my background, I wasn't used to being conned. In the army you could leave your money on the table with the door unlocked and know that it would be safe. You could trust your friends with your life. But once I'd got the money for my injuries, the letters started coming. 'You don't know me, but I've got a great idea, the only thing I need is some money, and you could be a partner in the business, bla, bla, bla...' And so I went into business, and got my fingers very badly burned.

I made lots of other mistakes. If a friend called by I'd drop everything and go out for a couple of pints without thinking twice. Looking back on it, those years were dark times. I nearly went bankrupt, almost lost my marriage, my new family, everything. That happened to a lot of friends who were in the Falklands, more than I realised at the time.

The difference between them and me was the support I got from my family. That saved me from a very dark fate, and I shudder to think what could have happened. Once I realised what was going on, what I'd almost lost, I started to control the drinking and put my life in order.

Denzil sold life insurance and worked as a financial advisor ('a very conscientious one, because of the lessons I had learned myself') until the financial crash in the late eighties made it a difficult field to be in. Then in 1990 came another unexpected blow, following on from the Falklands injuries.

I got very ill again - with something called Pseudomonas, an infection in the blood which had been lying dormant in my system since the injuries. It happened because of the soil and dirt that was blown into my body. It's a very crafty bug – it can lie there secretly for years before deciding to attack, as it did with me. It was only about a year before then that they'd found a treatment for it. It very nearly killed me, so I had been lucky now for a second time to survive my injuries.

Soon afterwards he was advised by the department of Government War Pensions that he was eligible to receive a pension covering a hundred percent disabilities resulting from his wounds.

I had been entitled to the pension from the day I left the army. Through the years when I was searching for ways to make a living the whole thing would have been completely unnecessary if I'd only had the right advice. The pension was very high because of the seriousness of my wounds, and my life started to improve dramatically without the stress of having to earn money. I felt now that I needed to give something back.

I'd been active for some years with the SSAFA – the Soldiers, Sailors and Airmen's Families' Association. And then around 1994 an old friend, who was working with the Army Benevolent Fund, asked if I had ever thought a Veterans' Association might be needed for the lads who had been in the Falklands. I said that it had crossed my mind, but that perhaps some high-ranking officer would be the one to get things started. He told me he thought I had the ability to do that myself. It was good to be told that, and I'd never even considered it. So I set about making contact with a number of people, including my old boss, Hew Pike, now a Major General, Tony Davies who was an RSM in the Welsh Guards, and Commander Jolly. Sarah Jones, Colonel H. Jones's wife, was also supportive. We held a little meeting at the General's house, and we launched the South Atlantic Medal Association in April 1997.

Denzil was the Association's secretary from the outset, working from home before opening the office in Pontllanfraith. Although he does not receive a salary, he works as hard as any of his neighbours on the industrial estate. Branches were opened in many parts of the world and by now the association has 2000 members. In 2002, twenty years after the war, a pilgrimage back to the islands was organized and Denzil was among the 240 members who made the journey.

I'd been lucky enough to return to the Falklands twice before that, and I knew how much good that had done me. Like many of the others I suffer from PTSD – Post Traumatic Stress Disorder. It used to be called shell shock or battle fatigue, or lots of other things, but after the Falklands it was labelled PTSD, defining a clinical condition which can be medically diagnosed.

SAMA has done a lot of work to bring the condition into public awareness, and to make sure that sufferers get help and treatment. The pilgrimage to the islands was a great help for people troubled by their memories of the war. Seeing the place at peace, beautiful islands with all their wildlife, is an excellent way of resolving turmoil left behind by what happened in 1982. Not to forget those things, but to look forward to the future without having to carry the heavy burden of wartime memories.

Unlike some PTSD sufferers, Denzil did not need residential treatment. He says that he received valuable advice from a psychologist in Cardiff.

The most important thing he showed me was that the feelings running through my mind weren't going to disturb anyone else. I was sure that none of my friends were having anything like these feelings, but he showed me that this was untrue, that this was something completely normal for people who have gone through strange and abnormal experiences. Thank God it's only a small part of the population that has to experience things like this. That's why we are soldiers in the first place, so that the rest of the population doesn't have to go through such things.

In 1993 Denzil made a journey even more unusual than his pilgrimage - to the capital of Argentina to meet up with some of the soldiers he had been fighting against.

A magazine called *La Gente* ('The People') invited a small group of us to Buenos Aires to meet some of our old enemies from the Seventh Infantry Regiment. The magazine would then write up the story of our meeting, as some sort of reconciliation I expect. I had my doubts about it from the start, but it was a chance to see the country, and I've always enjoyed travelling. We were only there for three or four days, and it proved to be a strange and very emotional time, meeting those we had been fighting against. We realised that we weren't just men obeying orders, nor were we particularly political people, nothing but straightforward soldiers. There was no hatred or lack of respect. We respected them, and they respected us. We found we could share experiences with them that we couldn't with anybody else - not even our closest family.

Unfortunately someone had decided that there had to

be armed guards accompanying us, in case other people who might object found out that we were there. But we sensed no threat whatsoever. I felt sorry for our former adversaries. They had been treated far worse by their government than we had. We met the families, we had a drink with them, there were tears and hugs and a great deal of fun - I'm still in touch with some of them.

We all agreed on one thing, that the war should never have been fought. And they agreed with us that the Argentinian government was to blame for all the suffering and loss of life, because they wanted to distract the country and the people's attention from problems at home. Reaching an agreement between Argentina and Britain is important now, as long as we don't compromise the islanders' right to decide their own destiny.

As I rose to go, Denzil said that he had to leave the office for a minute to look for a part for his motorbike. He noticed my surprise and explained that it was a three-wheeler, large, powerful - and which gave him great pleasure. I asked him if he had any other interests in addition to his work with ex-soldiers. Yes, he said, he had learnt to fly and had gained his pilot's licence, all after losing his leg and suffering all the injuries. 'Anything to do with speed,' he said, 'and I'm completely happy'. He enjoyed fishing as well, and had the opportunity to do that on his pilgrimage to the Falklands.

This was a man enjoying life to the full - the life he lost, for a brief spell, back then in 1982.

THE CONFLICT IN WELSH PATAGONIA

14. THE WAR CORRESPONDENT

Of all the television reports on the Falklands/Malvinas war there is one I won't forget, partly because it was me who decided to put it on air. Somewhere about half way through the programme Russell Isaac, the reporter from *Y Dydd*, can be seen at an asado (barbecue), among his young friends, waving a jug of wine in one hand. 'They're saying to me,' he says to camera, 'that there's some trouble going on to the south between Britain and Argentina. But here in Patagonia there's no problem with the relationship between the Welsh and the Argentinians...' To prove the point the wine flows and the whole gang unites in a resounding chorus of 'Salud!' and 'Iechyd da!'

Though the scene is more in the spirit of *Wish You Were Here* style travel TV than war reporting, I do not recall hesitating too much about including it in the programme. I thought of it as making a necessary point in the middle of the wall to wall jingoism, where the kith and kin argument was being used consistently to stir up anti-Argentinian sentiment. It is fair to say that my boss, Geraint Talfan Davies, was not in full agreement.

Looking back, sending Russell to Patagonia was probably quite a bold decision. Though the power of politicians to control news had not then been perfected to the degree it has today, the nature of the war made it harder than ever for

British journalists to be independent. The only way they could reach the conflict was on one of the task force's ships, and they were at the mercy of the military authorities. The main channel of news for most of us at home was a colouress and monotonous official called Ian McDonald, a spin doctor before his time, chronicling each day's events on the battlefield.

It became apparent, in spite of this, that the Argentinian propaganda machine was a hundred times more misleading. Compared to that even the Iraqi Minister of Information in the 2003 war would have sounded honest and plain-speaking.

In that thorny situation we sent Russell to Patagonia, to be among friends who were officially 'enemies'. He was even staying, while in Buenos Aires, at the home of a newly retired senior officer in the Argentinian army. The British authorities didn't even know he was in the country, let alone being in any position to influence his reporting.

Before joining HTV Russell had stayed in Patagonia for part of his university course in Bangor. He had won a scholarship to study the Welsh community in Y Wladfa for his MA in sociology and anthropology. He had learnt Spanish and made many friends there among people his own age.

Today Russell Isaac runs an independent television company in Bridgend specializing mainly in sports.

The Malvinas trouble happened within two years of me joining HTV after my research work in Y Wladfa. As far as I know I was one of the few people who could look at the whole trouble from the Argentinian viewpoint and from the Welsh viewpoint. During my year in Patagonia I had lived among the people, playing rugby and making friends as well as studying. So I got to learn Spanish, which gave me some sort of qualification to go back there, because I could communicate with people from that country who couldn't speak Welsh or English.

I became aware before going to Y Wladfa for the first time that there were some islands in the area called the Falklands but when I was there I'd have people asking all the time what I felt about the Malvinas. So this became something I had to find out more about and I did some research to understand the history, what had happened there and people's feelings about the islands. Because people were very emotional about them even at that time, and wanted something to happen. Nothing was happening from the British viewpoint of course, nothing at all. When the events of four years later took place it wasn't such a surprise to someone like me who had been there, because of that depth of feeling locally. Perhaps it was a shame, that way of trying to win the islands back, but one could see why they did it – this isn't to justify it, but to understand some of the reasons behind the whole thing.

When South Georgia was taken and the Argentinian forces landed on the Malvinas, I was working in Pontcanna with HTV. I remember going up to some of my colleagues in the canteen one Monday morning and one of them saying to me: 'You're the boy to go, since you've good connections with people in Patagonia. This isn't just a story that's world-wide, it's a story of exceptional relevance to Wales.' And I remember going upstairs to talk to you (Ioan Roberts) about it and then sitting down with the department heads, Cenwyn Edwards and Geraint Talfan Davies, and the two of them saying 'Yes, a good idea, we'll see how we can get you there.'

That's how it started. I went out there as the British armed services were preparing the task force to go. It had actually started on its journey, but no fighting had taken place. I was one of the last journalists to be allowed into Argentina, as they were closing the borders. ITN and the BBC were already there and, as we needed a cameraman and someone to help with the liaison, I got two of my old friends who lived in Argentina to do that, and the three of us worked on the news items.

At first I was in Buenos Aires and we started running items with Welsh Patagonians who lived in the capital. I was trying to work with the ITN boys, and realising that they had no great interest in what we were doing. They saw me as an oddity because I was reporting in Welsh, even though I was putting out items in English as well for *Report Wales*. They regarded the connection with the Patagonian Welsh as 'interesting' but not as something to be taken seriously.

Then we decided that if we were to get to the root of feelings in Patagonia we would need to go there. But there were problems getting the pictures back to Wales. At that time everything was being recorded on film, not video. ITN thought that their daily items were more important than our stories, and we weren't able to send our stuff back from Buenos Aires with theirs. We had a film editor with us, Viv Grant, who worked on the material in Buenos Aires - then someone would fly the film to Rio de Janeiro or Montevideo, and send it on to Britain by satellite link from there. Viv had to use a dreadfully old editing machine and our way of working was very crude. I was learning my craft at the time, and this was certainly a challenge.

It was interesting being there because I had

connections with the people and I wasn't part of the ongoing propaganda war. So I was able to do things that were different from what the other journalists were doing. The aim was not to try to compete with ITN and the BBC, who had the resources and teams to produce hard news reports. The timing of our work meant that nothing was being shown until at least four days later. So we had to make features more related to Wales. That's why it was appropriate to go down to Patagonia, and send items back that were separate and gave a different viewpoint on a situation that was deteriorating from day to day.

The conflict was causing no problems between me and my friends. We were all aware that this was a squabble between governments. They were in no way loyal to the Galtieri government. They'd had a belly full of the military being in charge, and were aware too that a conservative government was in charge under Thatcher in Britain. They believed that both sides were going to look for a fight. One way or another that was inevitable. That's what they felt at the time. Up until when the fighting started, I really thought that someone somewhere would intervene, that some sort of common sense would take over. A struggle had been going on for years between Argentina and Chile over the Beagle Islands. The Pope had intervened there to help reach a decision on what should happen to the islands. The United Nations had also become involved. Somehow or other I kept thinking something like that would happen - someone like the United States would turn around and say: 'Wow boys, this is stupid. You don't want to fight over all this.' I was completely wrong. Perhaps the clash was unavoidable because these were two governments fighting for their lives. Whoever won the war would retain the leadership in their own country.

What I was trying to do was show that there was another point of view, and something deeper involved than a political quarrel - that there were connections and relationships in Patagonia that went much deeper than the rhetoric of that time. Trying to show that we the Welsh had an extremely special connection down there and that the people there felt the same thing: that they saw Wales as separate from England, separate from Britain, and were trying to maintain their culture and their Welsh identity because of that historical connection. I don't want to over-romanticize, but that relationship still holds, like it or not. So all I was trying to do was to show to us, the people of Wales, on *Y Dydd* and on *Report Wales*, in Welsh and in English, that this connection remained, that there were people thinking in a different way, beyond the propaganda, beyond the rhetoric, beyond the jingoism.

I have been in the television business for over twenty years now and viewers still remember the period at the end of the programme *Y Dydd* when these items were going out. I believe they made an impression on people. S4C didn't exist yet. We were about the only daily platform taking any sort of viewpoint on the whole trouble different from what the dominant British spin allowed. And a lot of Welsh people still remember and appreciate what we were trying to do.

But not everyone liked that point of view, and it gave rise to some anxious reactions from the company's controllers.

I remember making an item in Buenos Aires trying to

explain the difference between the word Malvinas and the word Falklands. I made it standing by a clock tower given by the British government to Argentina in the century before last. To Argentinians the word Falklands didn't exist. They were the Malvinas and that was that. To us they were the Falklands and the Malvinas didn't exist. So through using the word Malvinas they were showing 'yes they exist and they belong to us.' The use of the word was important. I tried to say that Malfinas was a word we used in Welsh too for the Falklands, with an 'f' instead of a 'v'. But I remember being reprimanded for that because this edict had come out, a commandment from somewhere in London, that the word Malfinas/Malvinas wasn't to be used at all by journalists. Falklands had to be used every time in line with the war propaganda.

The second item that caused some controversy was the one down in Y Wladfa on the farm owned by one of my friends close to the Chubut River. I hadn't meant to record an item but the boys had invited me to an asado with them by the river after work. So we went, my two colleagues and I, the three of us having asado with friends. I thought doesn't this throw light on what's happening here, that the people of Argentina are about to go to war with Britain and here I am, a Welshman, with Argentinian friends as if the war wasn't happening at all. So I decided to throw an item together, an impromptu piece to camera, showing a group of us drinking wine, and showing that good relations between friends were going to last however bad things were between governments. So it was made, without our being sure it would see the light of day. But it was used. I recall that I recorded a piece to camera in English as well, but that one wasn't used!

Adopting a light tone in such a serious matter was something dangerous perhaps, against the prevailing current certainly, and they didn't want to show that we had friends there if we were in a war situation. That was the explanation I received later for the item not being broadcast in English - that it was against government guidance, that nothing was to be broadcast that could endanger the campaign by going against the grain.

Before the end of his stay in Y Wladfa Russell became part of the news himself. He was arrested by the Argentinian authorities on suspicion of spying.

After sending some reports from the Chubut Valley in the east, I felt I should go over to Cwm Hyfryd in the Andes to make one about the dispute between Chile and Argentina over the Beagle Islands. So we went over there and on one of our first days we were arrested when we were on the way to the border between Argentina and Chile, Fernando, myself and the cameraman, and put in the back of a wagon. They threw us in jail on suspicion of spying. What happened was that a *Sunday Times* journalist had been arrested further to the South in Comodoro Rivadavia, for taking pictures of an army camp. And the order went out for any other British journalists to be arrested if they were under suspicion. After imprisoning us for no reason they charged us with spying. Fortunately for us, Fernando's father was an ex-colonel in the army in Buenos Aires - otherwise I don't know what would have happened. We left them to phone him and after he had confirmed who we were they freed us, except that we were taken straight to the capital on the next flight from Esquel, with orders that we would not be allowed to go to the South where they were making preparations for war. So half way through our work we had to return to Buenos Aires.

We started producing some items there once again and by this time we were beginning to gain some influence with ITN. They were realising that I wasn't just a curiosity, that I spoke Spanish and had connections with the soldiers through Fernando and his father. Things were going very well.

But then, abruptly, I got a phone call in the middle of the night. It was Geraint Talfan Davies, speaking Welsh to begin with then switching to English because he was with someone who needed to understand what he was saying. The message was that I had to leave the next day, whatever the circumstances. I *must* leave. I tried to reason, that I wasn't in any sort of danger. If anything I was safer than the majority of the journalists who were out there. No! Advice had come from sources very high up in HTV that it was essential to leave. Something was about to happen and there was concern for my safety. That was the reason. I said that the only way I could leave the next morning was to catch a boat and cross the river, the Rio de la Plata, over to Montevideo. But once I was there is would be very difficult to get back into Argentina because they were refusing entry to people with British passports. But there was no reasoning with them. Leaving was the only course of action.

The next morning I got a boat straight across to Montevideo, reached Uruguay, tried to inquire about any possibilities of getting back. 'None at all' was the answer. The British Embassy was not to be reasoned with either. There was nothing useful I could do in Uruguay, while there were plenty of things I could have been doing in

Argentina. There was nothing for it but to fly home, a long and complicated journey through North America, Africa and Switzerland. I didn't get to return to Argentina. It had been a bit of an adventure, but at the time when it would have been most useful for me to be there I was back at home again.

When I left Argentina there were all sorts of rumours and anxieties around – that a nuclear bomb was going to be dropped, that the RAF was going to attack Buenos Aires, that they were going to target Cordoba. None of these things happened. But the next day saw the sinking of the *Belgrano*.

15. FOUR WELSH WOMEN

IRMA

One of the obvious places to look for a record of Patagonian people's experiences during the Malvinas war was in the columns of *Y Drafod*, 'the Welsh of Y Wladfa's local newspaper' – which, since it was founded by Lewis Jones in 1891, has faithfully chronicled the life and times of the community. This was a reason to visit the National Library of Wales and browse some of the 1982 editions. My hopes were raised by seeing a reference in one issue to a visit by my colleague Russell Isaac: 'He arrived... at the exact time when the St David Society was making its pilgrimage to the Valley of the Martyrs... Along with Russell Isaac came the arrival of a series of cassettes for learning country dancing...'

The only actual mention of the war that I could find was on page 11: 'A cloud came across our country with the fighting in the South. Despite that activities associated with the Welsh life persisted...'

And that's all. It may be that some experiences were too deep and personal to air in public, even in a local newspaper.

In Gaiman I called in to see Irma Hughes de Jones, the leading author and poet of Y Wladfa, and editor of *Y Drafod* for much of her life. Four or five years previously she had moved from her old home, Erw Fair farm in Treorcki, to live with her daughter Laura and niece Rebecca. I had some connection with the family as I knew Laura's husband, Phil Henry, a staunch and good-humoured Welshman from Llansamlet who lived for a while in Y Wladfa. Phil died at the age of 36 at Treforys hospital, on 13th of April 1982, when the British task force was on its way to the South Atlantic.

Irma was physically frail but in wonderfully good spirits, her memory a treasure house of community history. She was delighted to be talking about her roots in Wales, a country she had never lived in, and pointing to pictures around the room of places in the old country with which she had connections. Once or twice she sang songs she remembered from her young days. Nothing made me think this might be my last chance to meet her. Irma died three months later, on the 18th of April 2003.

I will have been editing *Y Drafod* for fifty years in May, if I'm alive and well. I'd like to be able to reach the half century, then perhaps someone else can take it on. I got so much pleasure from the work that I never used to tire of it. But I've started feeling tired now, at 84 years old. Before I came to Gaiman and got the computer I was writing it all by hand, cutting it up into little pieces with a scissors and pasting those on paper the right page size, taking it all to the printers.

We didn't pay much attention to the Malvinas war because it wasn't affecting us directly, although it did have an effect on a lot of us in other ways of course. We were very glad to see it over, naturally, because we didn't like to think that people were being killed. It was a very sad time. The son of a cousin of mine was there, having gone to fight on the British side, and he was lucky enough to return home afterwards. 'Back home without a scratch' he said.

I was in Wales soon after the war. It was an unpleasant feeling and I didn't want a lot of publicity about being there because I was some sort of enemy, wasn't I? Laura had lost her husband in April and they thought that the war might have upset Phil, because his wife and little girl were Argentinians weren't they, having been born here? He was terribly worried about that, and after breakfast that day he got up to put the radio on and fell to the ground – it was a stroke.

I wanted to travel to Wales then to see them but for months I wasn't able to go. In the end I went in December and was there for almost three months. What made things easier was that I had a British passport as well. What they told me in Buenos Aires at the embassy representing the old country was that I should use the Argentinian passport when getting on the plane to leave the country and afterwards use the other one. That's what I did of course. I landed at Gatwick airport and was trying to reach them at home, at Laura's place, to say I had arrived, but I couldn't get through. I asked some woman how to get out of there and she told me to follow the arrows so off I went outside. I got the bus to Swansea and I hadn't realized that British time was different from ours. Everywhere in Trelew is open until midnight at least but when I reached the bus station in Swansea it was half past ten and everywhere was shut. A man and a woman turned up from somewhere and I asked them what I should do to find a taxi. 'I'll phone' he said and I got a taxi to Llansamlet. They had changed the money not long before that and pound notes had gone out of existence. I didn't realise that. I gave an old pound note to the lad and he asked me 'Have you been saving love?' But I had some of the new pounds too and I paid him with one of those.

I'm glad that I was able to get to Wales that time. I did think about going again afterwards but the chance never came. And I couldn't go like this in a wheelchair could I.

It's that sort of thing I remember most about the war. What did I think of Thatcher and Galtieri? Oh dear me, I'd say that the two should have been sent to fight each other since they wanted a fight - that's what they should have done. 'Scatter the people who love to make war,' that's what the Bible says.*

RINI

Rini Griffiths is a woman of the mountains. She runs a hostel called *La Chacra* ('the farm') above Esquel in the Andes, and she makes you feel at home straight away there among her children, her grandchildren and their dogs. But she was originally a girl from the valley, having been born in the Bryncrwn neighbourhood near Gaiman. before venturing across the prairie to Cwm Hyfryd in 1963, as some of the early Welsh settlers had done almost a century before that. By now she maintains close contact with her family in Llanuwchlyn, even though there was a period of nearly a hundred years with no contact at all between the relatives in the two countries.

I didn't know that we still had relatives in Wales. I would ask Nain 'Are there no cousins anywhere in the Old Country?' 'Oh, I don't know,' she said, 'I never write to them.' There was nothing left for her in Wales, that was

---

* See Psalms 68:30

the feeling I was getting. Everything for her was here in Argentina.

Today Rini is one of those responsible for the revival of the language and of Welsh cultural life in Esquel. A modern Welsh Centre has been built next door to Seion chapel, following a long fund-raising effort. A nursery school, evening classes and all kinds of Welsh cultural activities take place there, and two fierce wolfhounds run back and forth along the flat roof, to keep mischief at bay. Framed on the wall inside is a line from the englyn to Mynytho Hall by R. Williams Parry: 'Built out of love not stone'. At the heart of all these activities is Rini.

> At the beginning they regarded it as something strange. They weren't accustomed to fighting for the Welsh language. No one actually denied that they were Welsh, or anything like that, but to make an effort or collect money – that was too much of a hassle. If we put a concert of some sort on at the chapel they wouldn't let us charge for entry. It felt like a sin to charge for getting into chapel. So we needed to have some kind of centre. We've got one now and everyone's very happy.

In this area bordering on Chile, and as far as you can get in Y Wladfa from the Malvinas and Buenos Aires, the war in 1982 didn't have much impact at the beginning.

> At first it was like some children's game for us. We didn't have much emotional connection to either side. We had no television at the time, because we lived a bit too far away where no cable reached, and we listened to the radio. Because we were so close to Chile, radio reception

from there was good for us. And Chile radio was saying something I would never have imagined, that Argentina was losing the war. We were listening to the radio from Chile saying that such and such number of Argentinians had been killed, then hearing Argentinian radio from Buenos Aires saying that everything was going very well and that it was our side that was killing everybody.

Very few from this area went to the Malvinas, and when you didn't know anyone over there very well the feelings weren't the same. We knew of one friend who had gone there and whose mother never got any letters from him. He was a little eighteen year old boy who had left school to learn to be a soldier, but wasn't really learning that. Only learning to march and to get to the camp on time. He hadn't even slept at the camp overnight, just gone to work in the morning, come home for dinner and back again in the afternoon. He didn't know how to kill a mouse or anything. And we wanted to help him because he was a friend, having been to school with my children and in the same skiing team. And we decided because this boy was so far away and his mother was so worried that we would send him a package each week with a little letter, all of us remembering ourselves to him - everybody getting together to help, one knitting a hat, another some woollen socks, one sending chocolate, another a little cake, things that wouldn't take up too much room, putting them in a box, taking that to the post office and sending it to the boy. We did that every week during the war, wrote very many letters, and put a little bit of money too in every box in case he didn't have any. But he never received even one package. Nothing ever. No letter, no chocolate, nothing.

In the end the boy came back, when everything was

over, and we heard what had actually happened. We didn't get the truth till perhaps two months or so after the thing ended. What the Chilean radio had been saying was true.

The boy's mother and father still live in Esquel but he has gone to work in Buenos Aires now.

IRIS

Her body is frail and illness has made her hands tremble, but her voice is strong and unwavering. It was in her cousin's house in Gaiman that I got to chat with Iris Sbannaus, but her home is in Buenos Aires. It was with Iris and her husband, a lieutenant colonel in the Argentinian army, that Russell Isaac ('our son from Wales') stayed during the war.

I was born into a Welsh family in the Andes, Dada and Mama having been born here in Argentina. Nain lived with us. She was Lewis Jones's daughter and Taid, Llwyd ap Iwan, was the son of Michael D. Jones. None of us knew Llwyd ap Iwan because he had been killed. But Mam would talk about her father all the time. She said that he was a modern man, and from what I've read about him since I would have liked to have known him, chatted with him. But there it is.

We were born in Cwm Hyfryd and lived there, in the Camp (farm) as we say, through the school years until we moved to live in Esquel. We spoke Welsh at home but I never learned to read and write in Welsh - so since then I remember the language we used to speak at home and because of that I don't keep the language up as well as I should. I haven't got enough words sometimes to say how I'm feeling and that makes me want to speak Welsh better than I do.

I got married in Esquel but because my husband was a soldier we lived all over, getting moved every couple of years. Because of that I know Argentina from one end to the other. But when he retired we went to live in Buenos Aires and that's where we've been for thirty years now. He isn't from a Welsh background at all. His father was from Germany and his mother from Spain. So our children are ... Americans! They're a little bit of everything. We are a big family, five children and all married – I've got fourteen grandchildren.

When the war broke out, I was working then, and I couldn't understand what they were trying to do. I had mixed feelings, you see. In some ways I thought it was good because now we would have the Malvinas, which was where they're supposed to be. And afterwards I thought what kind of war is this? I saw that it was something beyond all reason. And they told lies you see. We thought that things were going better than they really were.

After everything was over I saw the names of the boys who had been killed, so many of them. And to think they had done something like that so we wouldn't think about what was going on in the country. It's not easy to say what one feels because we do feel that the Malvinas belong to us. That's what we have learned and that's what we believe to be true. But afterwards sometimes I think what would we want the blinking islands for anyway - they are ugly and there's so much wind. And to tell the truth England never thought about the people of the Malvinas until this business came up. But afterwards they were *very important people*. And what Thatcher did to the *Belgrano*, that was beyond all reason and beyond all feeling. Letting them sink like that. Do you know, it's something I never talk about. I don't like talking about the Malvinas because it raises a feeling of rage and it's sad, unfair. But that's how every war is, from what I know.

I was working at the time. I'm a Mormon you see. We have an office in Buenos Aires - to look after the chapels, buildings and so on. I was working a lot, had a lot of responsibilities, and then the children were with me at home as well. I had a lot of work to do. And one of our children went to volunteer to go to the Malvinas but luckily they didn't accept him. Thank goodness it didn't turn into a long war - they won in a month or two didn't they.

I understood nothing about the war. Before it happened we knew the Malvinas were there and there was a lot of coming and going. We did all we could to help the people of the Malvinas. They had got planes – everything they had came from this country, they were getting nothing from England. And now after the war they are getting everything from the English.

My husband had retired before then but he wanted to go to the war. The whole thing was so unfair and stupid and bad. We study the history of the Malvinas in school and how they stole the islands at a time when Argentina didn't have enough of anything to get them back with. If you look at a map you see that there's a piece of land under water and the Malvinas are part of one land with Argentina, so they belong to us.

VALI

'Careful now! Nain is driving!'
You could have been in the company of any ten year old lad in Wales who's a bit disrespectful of his grandmother,

but we were in a pick-up outside *Tŷ Gwyn* in Gaiman, and it was Filipe who was speaking. 'Nain', Vali James de Irianni, has handed the Welsh language on to her children, even thought they were brought up in Buenos Aires and their father is not from a Welsh background. One of the sons, Ricardo, lives in Gaiman as well, and his children speak the language. Their family runs *Tŷ Gwyn*.

Though she has spent most of her life in Buenos Aires, Vali has stayed in close touch with her roots in the Chubut Valley, especially so through the time of the war.

I remember well the 2nd of April 1982. Of course we had understood since school days that the islands geographically and historically belonged to Argentina, but suddenly here we were hearing that Argentinians had landed there. We were astonished, of course, and believed there would be consequences. I'm not sure what the government here was expecting. But if you consider the history of Britain, taking each piece of land they felt like grabbing, and taking it without permission, there was every reason to think they wouldn't remain calm, that something major was going to happen in relation to the Argentinian landing.

We understood at the start that these marines were only going to the islands to show that we had a right to them, that we were capable of taking them back, and to stop there. Ordinary people don't understand what's happening between these countries, but we feared that the response from the other side wouldn't be a happy one.

Buenos Aires where we live was far away from the islands but Y Wladfa is close, isn't it, and we understood that all the to-ing and fro-ing would be in and from

Patagonia. Dada and Mama were there on the farm at the time, and getting old. Then our son, Ricardo, had just got out of the air force. He wasn't called up but I'm not sure what would have happened if the war had gone on any longer. It's clear that he would have obeyed the order had he been required to go.

But the whole thing affected Dada. He couldn't understand, and he couldn't get over it - that the war had come so close to him on the farm in Bethesda in the Chubut Valley. Immediately the family were saying to me: 'Mam, go to be with Nain and Taid.' And that's what I did, catch a flight to Chubut. And what an experience! We were warned before reaching the airport at Trelew that when we got off the plane we should not look to either side. You would want to see everything though, so I just peeked through the corner of my eye and I could see that they had raised a big embankment and that behind it there were sure to be war planes. And two soldiers were marching back and forth along the embankment in camouflage gear. It wasn't a good feeling at all.

And Dada was upset. We can't say for certain that this caused him to lose his life, in September 2002, but it had an effect on him for sure.

One consequence of the war was that neither the Welsh people nor ourselves were able to travel so freely between the two countries. Not that we had any hostile feelings towards the Welsh, of course, because it hadn't been their decision. But there were big problems for years with the paperwork, not being able to get visas and so on.

I don't believe the Malvinas are good for anything for Britain now – so much expense for them. But of course the standard of living of people who live on the Malvinas has improved as a result of the war. It has been different for us here because there are scars for us, aren't there.

We had never had a war before in our lifetime, although we knew about the first and the second world wars. A few years afterwards there were some Welsh people coming over here and in conversation we'd say occasionally things like 'Oh yes, Godre'r Aran choir came before the war.' They'd look shocked, and think we were talking about the two world wars. But it was the Malvinas we were talking about – the Malvinas was our own little war. For us there are definitely two eras, before the Malvinas and after the Malvinas.

16. THE CHILDREN'S WAR

The coffee bar at the *Chapter* centre in Cardiff. A fortnight before my trip to Patagonia I went there to prepare the way by meeting a young man who had just made the journey in the opposite direction. Walter Ariel Brooks is fluent in Welsh, so much so that he is a tutor, as well as being a research student, in the Welsh Department at the University in Cardiff.

We hadn't met before and *Chapter* was quite busy. But there was no need to guess for long: there was no mistaking the Latin complexion. He introduced me to his wife Geraldine, an Argentinian from Buenos Aires who was also busy mastering the Welsh language even though she has no family connection with Wales.

Walter Ariel Brooks was nine at the time of the Malvinas War. He was living in Comodoro Rivadavia, which is about two hundred miles from the Chubut Valley, therefore closer to the islands, and an important military centre. For that reason Walter's recollections of the war were more vivid than one might expect.

Welsh was my grandmother's first language, but she died when I was still a baby. Her family came from Penbedw in central North Wales, on her father's side, and from Neath on her mother's. So I didn't learn Welsh as a child, not until I was around twenty or twenty two years old. My grandfather doesn't speak Welsh but does speak English - because my grandmother married an Englishman in Patagonia. My father remembers, as a boy, going to eisteddfodau in the Chubut Valley. On my mother's side, in the North of Argentina, I have family which is more Spanish and with some roots in Italy as well. A little bit of everything then, like every Argentinian.

I was born in Comodoro, and though that's not very far from Trelew there is no Welsh ambience in Comodoro, as there is in the Chubut Valley. I think it's right to consider it part of Y Wladfa though, because many of the Welsh moved to work in the oil industry, the most important in the area, in Comodoro. My father worked in the gas industry but he has just retired and is delighted with that!

I will never forget the second of April 1982. We went to school and suddenly the headmistress came in and said to us: 'Well, you won't be having lessons today. You can go back home. Because today the army has won back the Malvinas. So this is a holiday for everyone.' And everybody was happy because we were missing lessons. We knew about the Malvinas - teachers always talk about the islands - but it wasn't a burning topic at the time. We knew about them but didn't concern ourselves with them at all. We were only happy because there were no lessons, and no more than that. But this was a shock for everyone. Nobody had expected that the army would go to the Malvinas. There was no reason to go to the Malvinas.

There were two important Argentinian airfields during the war, one in Comodoro Rivadavia and the other in Rio Gallegos in Santa Cruz province 800 kilometres further to the south. Rio Gallegos was the closest airfield to the islands, but the two were equal in terms of importance. So we were very worried about the war: there's a military hospital in Comodoro as well as the oil installations. We all thought the British would bomb Comodoro - to block the oil supply and because of the airfield being there.

I remember feeling that we were going through a very dangerous time. Every night we had to put out all the lights in the city. Everything was dark and in each neighbourhood someone was responsible for safety, going around the houses asking if everything was alright and reminding people of their duty to observe the blackout. We had to put a bed cover across every window. And I remember we'd go to the supermarket and buy as much food as we could in case there were shortages. Also we were thinking of moving out into the countryside to avoid the danger of being bombed. Fortunately nothing like that happened.

One night the sirens went off and the next morning we heard on the radio that British planes had flown over Comodoro Rivadavia. I don't know if that's true, but we were at risk. I also remember going to school with a bedspread and having safety practice sessions. The school bell would ring and we would all hide under the tables and cover ourselves with the bedspreads. The teachers said that's what we would have to do if the planes came and bombed us. In a way it was all like a game to us. On the other hand it was quite an anxious feeling. After going back to school we were free in the afternoon and I remember playing with the other children – pretending we were at war. This would happen close to the motorway and each afternoon we would see a load of lorries pass by full of soldiers, bombs and all kinds of things.

Some friends of the family were in the army at the

time, young and inexperienced boys. I know that the army in Britain is very professional and that even if young lads are sent to war they will have had experience. This wasn't the case with the Argentinian boys.

From all I have heard and can recall everybody at the time was in favour of the war and happy about it. But I realise now that as Argentinians we remember nothing. We have no memory at all. Because we were going through a terrible period then, the worst period in Argentinian history I'd say, the time of the military dictatorship when 30,000 people lost their lives, were 'disappeared'. Everyone knew that something was wrong but nobody was complaining. During the Malvinas war the football World Cup was happening in Spain, so the majority of people felt that Argentina was winning all over, on the football field and in the war. The biggest problem was that we were all being deceived by the military authorities. We were hearing on the radio and seeing on TV that Argentina was winning, even in May and June. We read newspapers that claimed we were winning. Later we realised that we had been looking at fake pictures of ships sinking. We were thinking 'We are winning the war and we'll be keeping the Malvinas for ever.' But then one morning in June we woke up to hear on the radio that the army had been defeated. We couldn't believe it.

The impact of the war varied between the different parts of Argentina. In Patagonia, though we were all pleased, we were also worried because we were close to the islands. But in Buenos Aires people weren't thinking of anything except the football. No one knew much about the islands and the war. Maradona was far more important. Geraldine my wife was at school in Buenos

Aires at the time. She has very few recollections of the war. Yes she remembers, but very little.

When you go to Patagonia you'll be hearing from people who still believe that it's important for Argentina to get the Malvinas back. The say that the Malvinas are part of Argentina and they dream of the day when the army returns there. I agree with the idea that the Malvinas are part of Argentina because they are so much closer to the country, and from the viewpoint of the history. The English have interfered everywhere around the world, so they have no right to say that the islands are part of Britain. That's my opinion anyway.

But I don't agree with the military government's policies. I believe that they started the war to hide what was happening in Argentina at the time, everything that was going wrong. They made a terrible mistake, sent people like lambs to the slaughter. After we lost the war nobody really wants to ask exactly what happened, what the truth is. I believe that everyone would prefer to forget and not think about it. Because on one side we have lost the war and on the other all of us, all the Argentinians, were deceived by the government, and it's hard facing the fact that we were both defeated and tricked. Galtieri, Videla and the whole crew who ran the country are still free. [Galtieri died in January 2003].* They were all put in prison after Alfonsin and the democratic government won the election. But afterwards they were pardoned and they're free. There is no justice in Argentina.

It causes huge pain whenever I think about Argentina. It's my country and I have many happy memories from my childhood. I think every day about my family, friends,

---

* Videla died in prison in 2013

the atmosphere and way of life – and I miss all those things. It's very sad but it's hard to imagine a good future for me and my wife in Argentina unless some major change happens in the country.

17. THE WAR IN COMODORO

'This place here was very busy. This is where they brought the young soldiers to sort them out for moving south and on to the Malvinas. They were only children. It was at home with their mothers they should have been, not being sent out there to fight. And what the hell for?'

John Benjamin Lewis, or 'Benja', was driving me slowly in his Rover along the road that circled Comodoro Rivadavia air base, so important to the Argentinian war machine in 1982. Though this is the civil airfield servicing the city, the military presence is still very apparent: armed soldiers guarding the gates in the fence, a training camp next door and the soldiers' homes across the road. Benja and I concur that it would be unwise for me to get out and take pictures.

My chat in Cardiff with Walter Ariel Brooks had made me want to visit Comodoro Rivadavia. After inquiring with friends when I was in Gaiman, I telephoned Benja Lewis, originally from there, who had moved to Comodoro in the 1950s looking for work. Though he had no idea who I was, a pressing invitation to stay in his house followed. I set out from Trelew early one morning for a five hour journey by bus. The 'monotony of the pampas' may be a cliché but the fact is hard to escape. Whenever I surfaced from dozing and opened my eyes, the same flat landscape, with its patches of vegetation, stretched endlessly to the horizon in all directions - as if the bus had not moved an inch and the scenery was rushing past through some trick of technology. The only variation was the occasional gaucho on horseback, giving a friendly wave as if the bus was one of the highlights of his day. It was like travelling from Holyhead to Cardiff on a dead straight road and seeing no sign of habitation anywhere on the way.

The first indication that we were getting somewhere was the occasional oil pumping machine by the roadside, arms slowly moving with no human nearby. Then rows of rounded sandy dunes appeared on our left, affording glimpses of the sea in between. We were on the outskirts of Comodoro Rivadavia, Patagonia's largest city with a population of 130,000.

It was the oil industry that drew most of the families there, and that's what occupied Benja Lewis for most of his working life. He gave me an enthusiastic welcome at the bus station, and took me to his home which was behind a petrol station called *Eureka*, on a strip of land between mountain and sea. He explained that he had moved here from the Chubut Valley in 1952 after being apprenticed as a carpenter. He had a photograph of a bardic chair he made at the age of eighteen for Y Wladfa's eisteddfod. He worked as a carpenter in the cement works in Comodoro before getting a job with the oil company, and finally buying the petrol station now being managed by his son. His forebears had come to Y Wladfa from Blaenau Ffestiniog. 'I still have a friend who lives there. I don't recall his name, but I know he's a preacher!'

He took me on a tour of the city, which has some distinguished buildings, signs of wealth I had not previously seen in Patagonia. But there were also acres of industrial skeletons left by the large oil companies as they turned their backs on the area and headed for more profitable wells in Santa Cruz further south. Comodoro has three Malvinas War memorials within a hundred yards of each other on the beach, one for each branch of the armed forces. In front of the Army memorial to the soldiers who fell, a local woman was leaning on her stick. She peered at the names for some time before turning away and making the sign of the cross. I couldn't help taking a picture of her from a distance. After she left, it was our turn to look at the names. Perhaps one of them had been her son? Benja drew my attention to the Clase 62 or Clase 63 before each name. All had been born in either 1962 or 1963. And all had died in 1982.

Apart from the airfield, the place most affected by the war was the infirmary, the Hospital Regional. According to Benja that had been very busy:

> There was a lot of coming and going at that time. It was to here that they brought the soldiers wounded in the Malvinas. At the end of the war many people came looking for their boys. When a plane landed from the Malvinas, no one was told who was on it. People would ask and ask, with no one telling them anything, so they could do nothing except wait and keep asking and still hope.

The Welsh language has seen a resurgence in Comodoro. Some of the teachers from Wales living in Gaiman travelled to the South to provide lessons for beginners, and this gave a rare opportunity to Welsh speakers like Benja for practice in the language they rarely get a chance to use. He took me to a centre on the outskirts of Comodoro, built by the Welsh for Saint David's Day celebrations and other gatherings, with a round fire pit outside for asado. In the foyer there are pictures cut out from a 1970s calendar showing scenes from the Old Country. On one of the walls there is a row of coats of arms of the old shires of Wales. Everything here, including the building, comes from a hard labour of love performed by the Argentinian Welsh of Comodoro, exiled not only far from Wales but also from Y Wladfa, Behind the stage is a mural depicting a Welsh castle on one side and the Patagonian coast on the other. On the sea between them, the *Mimosa* sails in one direction, while a dove of peace flies in the other.

That evening Benja took me to meet the artist who created the mural. Originally from Trelew, Lila Hughes de Gastaldi was a retired teacher with roots in Blaenau Ffestiniog and Aberdare. She told me that painting was her hobby, and her commitment was evident from the number of her paintings everywhere in her house, in central Comodoro. She looks like an artist, and talks with a fiery directness especially when the topic of the Malvinas arises. Over supper in a restaurant near the harbour, I had the opportunity to question both Lila and Benja, two Argentinians who hold Wales very close to their hearts, about the Malvinas war. Lila was the first to tell me that the Argentinian authorities were suspicious of some of Y Wladfa's Welsh during the war.

Lila

It was a very sad time for the Welsh in Y Wladfa and strange things were happening. My father and mother were elderly people on the farm in the Chubut Valley, and their 'friends' (she makes quote signs with her fingers) who were in the Army would visit them. They would ask 'Whose side are you on?' They would reply 'We are

Argentinian and so were our fathers.'

Here in Comodoro things were very bad. I wanted to go to Buenos Aires to see my son who was studying there. The planes weren't flying from the airfield here because of the war, so I had to drive to Trelew initially and there were no lights to be seen anywhere. They were threatening to send my son to the Malvinas and I thought that perhaps this would be the last time that I would see him. At the time he wanted to go to the islands. His secondary education had been at a military academy here, and he was more experienced than the children they were sending to the Malvinas. Luckily, he didn't go. Why did he want to go? He said to me 'what will I tell my children when they ask "Where were you Dad, during the Malvinas war?"'

We all supported the thing at the time, but learned later that it was all lies. There's something soft in the head about the Argentinian. He'll happily believe politicos and believe the military - but they are not to be trusted.

Benja

The awful thing was the thought of a young boy, a son of the Welsh here, going to war and knowing that there were other young Welsh boys coming to fight against them. It's a very sad thing for us on both sides. We worried for ourselves and for the Malvinas. The whole affair was very painful for me.

Lila

I would go up to the roof occasionally during the war and look out across the sea, imagine that I could see the mountains of the Malvinas. I couldn't of course because they were too far away. We were told very little of what was happening, and most of that was lies to make our side look big and strong.

I still think now of Mrs Thatcher's situation, not as the chief lady, but as a woman, as a mother. I don't know how she can sleep at night, how she can live, knowing that she gave the order to sink the *Belgrano*. The very worst thing was the *Belgrano*. Deliberately killing people, regardless of who they were or where they were.

In 1985 we went to Europe, and my husband didn't want to visit London. He wasn't at all happy in London, but he felt much better after seeing 'Malvinas Argentinas' painted on a wall - there of all places! I believe by now that things are more stable, but for many years afterwards I thought of my life in two parts, before the war and after the war.

I know that we own the islands but I don't think too much about it by now. Our government can't look after our country here properly at the moment, let alone the Malvinas.

Benja

Before to the war there was a sort of connection between here and the Malvinas. Planes flew from here with fresh fruit and stuff for them. Anyone who wanted to go, could go, exactly as if we were at home, and the islanders could come here to the hospital. Now, since the war, nobody goes back and forth.

They said after the war that we had lost the Malvinas. We the Welsh had lost something else of great importance though. We were afraid that we had lost friends from Wales, and we were wondering 'what do they think of us now?' We hadn't started the thing, of course. That was people far worse than us.

Lila

And here we are now, with a lot of coming and going between the two countries. We are very glad that children from Comodoro can go to Wales to study Welsh, and children from Y Wladfa, some from Trelew and Gaiman, are starting to marry boys and girls from Wales. I think of that as a kind of present for us, after everything we've suffered before because of the war.

18. ON 'ENEMY' TERRITORY

While the Argentinian Navy played its part in the unsuccessful attempt to retake the Malvinas, one of its former members faced a different challenge - organising the Urdd National Eisteddfod being held that year in Pwllheli. Elvey MacDonald was quite possibly the most famous Argentinian in Wales at that time. The last thing on his mind when he came to live in Wales in the 1960s was that one day he might witness a war between the old country, Wales, and the country of his birth.

Elvey has since retired from his work with the Urdd, but he still lives near Aberystwyth. Born in Gaiman, he has a very personal reason for remembering the Malvinas war. That was when his mother, in her seventies, was interrogated on 'enemy' territory, suspected of being one of Galtieri's spies.

During the first attack, on South Georgia, Mum was in the air on her way to visit us in Aberystwyth. I had gone to Heathrow Airport and was waiting for her in Arrivals but there was no sign of her. I was thinking that she might have missed her flight, or that something had gone wrong, but actually she had been there all along, held upstairs and being interrogated by officials. Eventually I was paged over the loudspeaker and went up to where they were holding Mum. There was no smile or any warmth on the faces of these officials. They wanted to know first of all that I knew this woman and then that she was my mother. Then they started a cross-examination. Why was she going to Wales? What was her business there? Was she intending to stay there? Was she aware of the political situation? Through all this she was sitting on her chair and I wasn't allowed to go to her, even to hug her. I tried to explain that the visit had obviously been arranged prior to any signs of conflict - she was on the plane before it started. And she was hardly going to start spying at 71, in Aberystwyth of all places! Eventually they allowed her into the country.'

Elvey says that hearing about Argentina's attack on the Malvinas had been a 'shock and a disappointment' at the time. He had known all his life that there was a sense of national injustice about the islands. He later came to realise that the existence of Y Wladfa in Patagonia could historically have influenced the circumstances leading to the conflict.

Every child was taught, as part of the educational curriculum, about the invasion on New Year's Day 1833 and that the state had made a case for the islands to be returned annually since then. We would look at the map, see how near they were – on our continental shelf, not out in the far ocean - and that they were thousands of miles away from the country which claimed legal sovereignty over them. The question of the Kelpers' wishes just didn't cross our minds! The only thing we heard was 'They are close by, part of the land that was inherited from Spain'. For us in Chubut that interesting, because it's possible that this land might not have been part of Argentina at all had not the Welsh arrived and founded Y Wladfa. Our part of Patagonia was not shown on any map when Y Wladfa was founded in 1865. Prior to that the map of Argentina ended at the Rio Negro with nothing to the south claimed by anyone – so the islands were part of the unclaimed lands. The presence of the Welsh secured that land as part of Argentina. Of course we never got into the detail of that argument in school!

Elvey had been a dry land sailor during his military service, already in the Navy for two years before going near the deck of a ship. He was trained as a telegraphist, spending his second year at a radio station in Trelew, sending out weather reports and such bulletins to shipping. Prior to military service he had been following a teacher training course. One experience from the navy days stood out for him, illustrating the diversity of backgrounds among those thrown together in military service. This also became apparent with regard to Argentinian forces in the Malvinas.

I didn't like the Navy one bit. It was an alien experience for me and I did not enjoy the atmosphere. At a training centre in Bahia Blanca city, when I was there, they had a school for soldiers who were illiterate. Many of them had no more than a year or two of school behind them, having been brought up perhaps in the rainforest – many from Buenos Aires too, having left school aged ten before completing their primary education. So the special school at the centre was dedicated each evening to teaching them. One of their teachers fell ill and five of us in our group had recently completed teacher training. We were asked for volunteers and I was chosen to become a teacher of my contemporaries. Talk about teaching experience - I never, ever went back to education after that!

At that time both the Russians and the Americans were launching satellites, some of them manned, and these were visible to us occasionally in the evenings. They were like shooting stars, but slower, and they became less visible as the sun they reflected disappeared. These lads I was trying to teach had no interest at all in arithmetic and even less in writing. We had a strict curriculum we were supposed to follow, but who would notice? So I told them one night that we would study something completely new, about satellites and such like. There was no response, a total blank. I realised that they knew nothing about the solar system. Some struggled with the fact that the world was round. 'When you're on parade tonight,' I said, 'keep a look out for any satellites going past.' All the big lads sat at the back of the class, and when I said that there were men in space, that was too much! The biggest of them got to his feet and rushed to the front where I stood on a small stage, and clambered up intending to punch me. I stepped back in alarm and the other lads came forward to hold him back, because it was obvious that he was serious. A lot of them continued to disbelieve what I had said about space.

The idea was that those who had gone through training would form a military reserve in any future crisis. But Elvey had left the land of his birth long before the first real war in Argentina's history. He arrived in Wales for the first time in 1965, the first in a group who came over for three months to celebrate the centenary of Y Wladfa. At the end of this period he was invited to study Welsh at Coleg Harlech, the first of many students from Chubut to do so. He returned to

Patagonia at the end of his course but came back to Wales in 1968 to work for the National Eisteddfod, with the intention of staying for three years. At the end of that time he married his wife, Delyth, and here he remains. He had already put down deep roots in the land of his forefathers when news came in 1982 that the Argentinian armed forces in which he had served were trying to recapture the Malvinas.

I would have never foreseen such a thing. We had the problem at Heathrow with my mother, but apart from that I don't think there was any ill feeling while she was here. My children, however, were affected. At the time Camwy Prys was 12 years old, Meleri Mair was 11 and Geraint Llyr was 6. They had no problems at all in the Welsh schools in Aberystwyth, but outside school some harsh things were said, with kids their age calling them all sorts of names. The one that sticks in my mind, because it was so funny, was 'Argie Pants'! This didn't leave any scars at all. I think they were able to see the comical side of things. Also we never tried to bury the problem. We made it plain that the war was happening and what our viewpoint was, and we stressed the need to not get involved, not argue or fall out with anyone.

I remember being invited during the war up to Caernarfon to address a group of people in a pretty crowded room. Dafydd Wigley from Plaid Cymru and Emlyn Sherrington from the Labour Party were the other speakers. I was anxious about being there because I didn't know what to expect, but I was warmly welcomed. I said from the start that I wasn't sure why I had been invited other than perhaps to represent the enemy! I wanted to establish at the outset that I was an Argentinian, but I had no problem. And I didn't experience any problems during the whole time.

But not everyone was so lucky. There were two Argentinian ladies I knew of who were living in Wales at that period. One was a laboratory technician – she was given a terrible time by her fellow workers, and they were a group of scientists! They refused to speak to her and all sorts of things. The other was a Spanish teacher. When she first walked into the classroom all the pupils had their heads on their desks, refusing to raise them. Then they rose to their feet, sang *God Save the Queen* and then kept their heads down again for the rest of the lesson. That's how it was for her for quite a while, if not till the war was over. To tell the truth, these were very dark days for the people of Y Wladfa.

Unforseen consequences of the war went on for years, as Elvey was to discover.

It was very difficult to travel between the two countries at first. It affected me in an unexpected way as recently as the end of the '80s. I travelled to Brussels with a delegation from the Urdd, and on the way out I had no difficulty. On my way home the officials at the desk at Heathrow asked me, as they checked our passports, 'Where's your re-entry visa?' A visa was not needed on the way out, and no one had asked for anything in Brussels. We were flying with Sabena, and I was told afterwards that they had been fined a thousand pound for flying me out without warning me about the need for a visa to return. All this merely because I had an Argentinian passport. Argentinians needed entry visas to get into Britain for about ten years after the war. I believe all this came to an end about the same time as Rod Richards (the Welsh Office Minister) visited Y Wladfa.

How does Elvey regard the conflict 21 years later? He thinks and smiles before answering.

I remember the barber saying as he was half way through cutting my hair: 'Leave them to the penguins!' He believed that every living soul should be removed from the islands and that no flag should fly there. I feel that it's not worth losing even one life over the place, but I would have liked to see the United Nations judging who should own it. In the back of my mind I think that the most reasonable outcome would be for the islands to be governed by Argentina. Having said that, the Argentinian government hasn't excelled itself in the past in the treatment of its own citizens, so perhaps a handover period would be needed to make sure that people could keep their rights and so on. I do think that in the long run they should be under Argentinian rule. Best of all, if Patagonia became independent, they could be part of Patagonia!

It was obvious that both Thatcher and Galtieri did what they did to improve their own ratings in the opinion polls. When you think about the effects of that -Thatcher getting all those extra years in government, and Galtieri losing his grip on Argentina, resulting in the return of democracy - then I think that Argentina, all in all, got the better result.

THE PRICE

19. TECKA

There is a monument in the form of a marble wall in central Buenos Aires, put up to commemorate the Argentinians who fell in the Malvinas. It is guarded day and night by two members of the armed forces. Among its six hundred and fifty names, none would immediately strike anyone as being Welsh. Only someone with knowledge of the Welsh families of Y Wladfa would recognise the name Ricardo Andres Austin. To grasp the significance of that name one has to look at another memorial stone, six hundred miles further to the south.

That memorial, by the sea in Puerto Madryn, lists those pioneers who arrived there from Wales on the *Mimosa* in 1865. Because the names are arranged alphabetically, the first two belong to Thomas and William Awstin. They were orphaned brothers from the Aberpennar area, Thomas being 11 and William 14 years old. Some time later down the generations the Welsh 'Awstin' was Latinised to 'Austin', even though phonetically they remained the same. Thomas Tegid Awstin, the younger brother, was the great grandfather of Ricardo Andres Austin.

By all accounts the two young brothers had led quite a hard life even before boarding the *Mimosa*, working in the coalmines of Cwm Cynon. Looking after them during the voyage was an old family friend, Daniel Evans, whose own three year old son was also on the ship. That son, John Evans later known as 'Baqueano', became one of Y Wladfa's most famous adventurers and leaders. He was the young man who escaped, when held by local indigenous people, mounted on a horse named Malacara. This was after his friends had been killed in Dyffryn y Merthyron.

Thomas Tegai Awstin also became a prominent figure in the life of Welsh Patagonia. He was a member of Rawson's Town Council, and the first director of the Camwy Trading Company, before moving to Cwm Hyfryd in the Andes where he was one of the founders of Seion Chapel in Esquel. He and his wife Mary Williams had ten children. Today one of his great grandchildren, Jorge Austin, runs a tea shop called *Melys* in Esquel, and is one of the most active supporters of the Welsh Centre there. Another relation is Elvira Moseley who lives in Aberafan. Then known as Elvira Austin, she studied in Coleg Harlech in the 1960s and became a well known singer.

I accompanied Vali James de Irianni and her husband Jorge in their pick-up across the pampas from Gaiman to Cwm Hyfryd. That 400 mile journey involved none of the hardship or excitement of the one which faced the Welsh settlers of old, nor the monotony of my earlier journey taken as part of this trip between Trelew and Comodoro. The Chubut River runs alongside you for much of the way, the road tunnels through striking sandstone rock, and Dôl-y-Plu and Rhyd-yr-Indiaid are interesting places for a break in the journey. Before arriving in Cwm Hyfryd we had to make one important call. The first village of any size on the journey, only reached after hours of travelling, is Tecka. Here you can see the Andes in the distance and there are some signs of more fertile land ahead – but not quite yet. At one time the area caused some excitement among the Welsh when gold dust was discovered in the hills nearby. But Tecka never became a Klondyke, and the last thing anyone would associate with the village today would be wealth.

Despite the apparent poverty of many of the streets, the school (with its School No.17 sign) looks modern and bright. We were here to visit a woman who works there and lives in the same street. Celinde Espinoza de Austin was at the gate waiting for us. She was the mother of Ricardo Andres Austin, the young man of Welsh Patagonian lineage who lost his life in the Malvinas. Her partner was disabled and sat in front of the television, with children and mischievous grandchildren all around, determined to be helpful in every way. This was the one situation during the whole trip where I most regretted not having made a greater effort to learn Spanish before leaving Wales. Celinde looked straight into my eyes as she spoke of her son, with a quiet and gracious composure which helped me sense her meaning even without literally understanding her words.

She explained, through Vali, that it was only a few weeks earlier that she had started to receive the war pension due to her from the state in compensation for losing her son. This was in November 2002, twenty one years after the war. Also only recently arrived was the official report describing the circumstances of his death in the battle of Darwin and Goose Green. But she was glad to receive that report, bleak as it was:

'Sergeant GARCIA and privates AUSTIN and ALLENDE were selected to approach and silence the English machine-guns with their own MAG automatic weapons. In order to accomplish this they had to cross barbed wire obstructing their path on both sides. There they were exposed and fell under machine-gun fire. The two privates were killed in that action ...'

Vali told Celinde that I had met the parents of the boy from Llanberis who lost his life on the other side in the war. 'I hope they found the same strength that I did to face the situation,' she said.

One of the children clambered on to a chair to pass me a picture of Andres in uniform. They competed to get their hands on things to show us, articles and certificates chronicling his adventure in the Malvinas. Among these was a plastic medal acknowledging his bravery. His mother began to tell the story of the son who did not come home:

We used to live in my father in law Jorge Austin's house in Trevelin. my husband, myself and our four children. My mother-in-law's name was Mary Hughes but I never knew her. When my husband died we moved to Tecka. Here in School Number 17 all the children had their education.

One married daughter lives in Mar del Plata and another runs a shop in Trelew. Andres stayed home mostly to work on the land, but when he was eighteen he went to do his military service in Sarmiento. On 1st February 1982 he enlisted in the 25th Regiment, Sarmiento Infantry. On 29th March he sailed for the Malvinas. The intention was for them to land there on 2nd April, but because of technical problems they were held back. So they landed by helicopter on April 4th. He stayed there until 28th May, when he was killed in the battle of Darwin on the Goose Green peninsula. So he had been in the Army for four months, two of those in the Malvinas. He sent us some of the news in his letters.

In all, he sent us four or five letters. He was asking me to send sweets, chocolate, cakes and warm clothes. He was complaining that they weren't being told what was happening in the war, and they weren't being allowed to tell their families what was going on around them. But he did suggest to me that he was experiencing really horrific things. He said in his last letter from Darwin that he and his fellow soldiers had been ordered to leave in lorries. They had no idea where they were going or what was happening. I went to the Malvinas afterwards to visit the graves and they told us that the battle of Goose Green had started at the break of dawn on the 27th of May. Andres died the following day. They said that this had been a very tough battle, one of the hardest of the war.

At the end of the war I heard nothing about him, and had no idea what had happened to him. I would go to the police to ask if anyone knew anything, but still I heard nothing. It was July before I was told that he had been killed. Two months had gone past, and that's when a letter arrived from the Lieutenant in Sarmiento. He described seeing Andres rushing towards the enemy's machine gun and then seeing him fall. Quite a few other parents received similar descriptions of their sons at that time, only for some of those sons to turn up alive later on.

Someone from the Regiment in Sarmiento came here to see me, and to invite me on a trip that had been arranged to the Malvinas. There was a group of 21 of us on that visit, with a guide who showed us the different places on the islands. I saw the place where Andres was killed, and we visited the graveyard. But it wasn't possible to find him. There were no names on most of the graves. I believe there were 234 graves in all, of young soldiers, lieutenants, pilots. There were very few names.

Our guide gave us a description of the soldiers' conditions. They were cold, hungry and in a piteous state he said. Their clothes were lightweight and unsuitable, and the food and warm clothes we sent them did not arrive. The parcels were getting as far as Puerto Argentino and there they remained.

On the same trip, we went to Buenos Aires, where Andres's name is recorded among those who gave their lives for the Republic in the Malvinas. They promised us that we would be able to return to the Malvinas at any time in the future to visit the graves.

He was the only one from Tecka who went to the war. He said in one of his letters that he was happy to go to the Malvinas to fight for the Republic. They promised years ago that they would put up a memorial to him here in the village, but that has not happened yet.

20. LLANBERIS

There's no harsher work for journalists than knocking on the doors of people in the immediate aftermath of some disaster and trying to find a civilised way of asking them how they feel. More often than not they will never have met the people suffering and bereaved before and any expression of sympathy is going to sound fake. But it was in these exact circumstances, on the TV programme *Y Dydd*, that one of the most memorable interviews of the Falklands war took place. A family from Llanberis had just heard that their son, Raymond, was among those lost in the sinking of the *HMS Ardent*.

'What went through your minds?' asked the reporter. 'I'll tell you honestly,' said Raymond's father through his tears. 'We thought about the parents of the young boys on the *Belgrano*. Four hundred of those have been killed.' 'Such a loss,' said Raymond's mother. 'Yes,' said his father. 'And I see it as a loss for nothing'.

John Raymond Roberts was a twenty four year-old chef. He was one of the 23 who lost their lives when the Argentinian air force attacked the *Ardent* on 21st May near San Carlos between the two main islands. He was the second of Thomas John and Eileen Roberts's three children. Today Mr and Mrs Roberts still live in the family home at the foot of Snowdon next door to the station for the train that goes up the mountain. But there's more of a sea voyaging than a local mountain ambience in the living room: a 'Monarch of the Glen' stag tapestry on the wall, an Italian tramp figurine, and lots of little souvenirs from other countries on the shelves - showing that this was once the home of a sailor and a thoughtful one at that.

The parents haven't changed a lot in their appearance or their attitude in the twenty one years that have passed since then. It is clear with this welcoming and chatty couple that they never allowed their grief to turn to bitterness. The gracious spirit shown in that television interview remains here with them still.

Thomas John Roberts

It was a Saturday afternoon, and I'll never forget it. I'd got a job as a curator in the slate museum in Llanberis, after having worked in the quarry myself for years. I was working that day and there was a football match on the telly. 'Twm,' said one of the lads, 'Can you get a picture on this so we can watch the game?' We had a little old portable there and I went and started fiddling with it. But when the picture came on it wasn't the football they were showing but a news flash saying that the *Ardent* had been hit. That's how I first heard.

Eileen Roberts

I'd gone to Caernarfon to buy chips for us for dinner. After I got home the parson, Alun Jones, called by to say that Raymond was missing. The parson was the head man of the village in a way. He came back later to tell to us that Raymond was one of those who'd been killed.

TJR

The parson wanted pictures of him, cuttings from

newspapers and so on. He intended to create a scrapbook and to keep it in the church, even though we are chapel people. This happened in May, but by October the parson himself had died – he'd been murdered.

TJR

He was 16 years old when he went to the Navy. Although I'd been in the Army myself and seen terrible things, I didn't think about war when he joined. Raymond never thought about war at all during the whole time he was in the Navy. It was to the Empire Games that he was supposed to be going when he was sent to the Falklands, as escort to one of those big ships. He had seen quite a bit of the world.

He was dreadfully unlucky to be on the *Ardent* at all. He was on the *Southhampton* earlier on but got transferred because the *Ardent* was short of chefs. He had been with her for six weeks altogether. There was a young boy from Conwy with him, whose name was Tony. 'I'll look after him,' Raymond said to Tony's mother before they left.

ER

He had intended leaving the navy but after his marriage broke up he decided to go back for one more tour. When he was home on his last leave he had just been to Norway on some courtesy call. They had held a ceremony above where the last *Ardent* went down in a fjord around 1943. There had been three or four other ships called *Ardent* since then. That was the last thing he did before heading for the Falklands.

On the way out they stopped at Ascension Island first. He wrote us a letter from there telling us not to worry about him. He had been used to writing to us in English and this was the first time he wrote in Welsh. He said he was as brown as a berry because it was so hot there. But as they went nearer to the Falklands it was terribly cold. Even then we didn't think there would be a war. But we had a relative living across the road who had a son on the *Ark Royal*. She made us start thinking that things could turn bad.

TJR

The *Ardent* was a warship, ' Frigate Type E22' or something. They were to provide the cover if soldiers landed somewhere. But they had taken some of the missiles off the ship because they were too expensive. They only had the Exocets on the ship. They were sitting ducks to be honest.

We got a letter saying that a 1000 pound bomb had gone through the ship. Raymond was on fire duty when he got killed. The chefs had to do something else as well as cooking. And that was what he had chosen. Only one was killed by the first strike. Then the second came. I heard the pilot who sank the *Ardent* talking on television some time afterwards.

I think it was Margaret Thatcher who committed the great evil sinking the *Belgrano*. That's when things started going from bad to worse. Until then there was some hope of settling things. They had made a circle hadn't they, territorial waters in a way, and the ship was on its way home. That's what made the big difference, sinking that one. I wrote a letter to Tam Dalyell (the Scottish Member of Parliament opposed to the war) about that and got a very nice letter back. 'She sank the *Belgrano* while she was drinking pink gin at Chequers,' he said once.

But I felt terrible for the families over there. To think that there were just about 400 of them. I often think, you know, that Margaret Thatcher went into the Falklands to win the election. And it worked, she flew back in didn't she?

ER

When we went to the memorial service at St Paul's there was a buffet afterwards at the Guildhall and we saw the captain of the *Ardent* there. All the important people were there.

TJR

Everybody except the Queen...

ER

The Queen was there!

TJR

I didn't see her!

We saw the captain of the *Ardent* and the captain of the *Antelope*, which got hit on the same day. I enjoyed myself with the captain of the *Antelope*. He was saying how he felt terrible that the boys had gone down and he hadn't. In the old days the captain would have been the last one on the ship, but that doesn't happen with this lot.

We saw the parents of some of the other boys at St Paul's. And we got very many letters from them. A lot of them only had one son and had lost him. It was worse for them. We saw the father of the boy who was lost on the *Glamorgan*...

ER

We weren't the same for a long time after. We couldn't sleep or anything. But we had to carry on with our lives for the other children. They wouldn't have tried if we hadn't.

TJR

Our Member of Parliament, Dafydd Wigley, came to see us straight away. He had experience of it didn't he, having lost two sons. People from the newspapers were calling us all the time. Strangely the most decent of them was the man from the *Daily Mail*. Some of the others were like they'd come to take wedding pictures.

I should think that the whole thing has told on our children even more than it did on us. Raymond had an older brother, Reg, and a younger brother and sister, Ronnie and Iona.

ER

Iona was only 14 years old at the time and she hasn't mentioned it since he was killed. She can't talk about it. When someone came here to see us she would go to her bedroom out of sight. She was a baby when he was a big boy and he doted on her. He would bring back dolls for her from wherever he went. He was unbelievably kind.

TJR

The thing has made a world of difference to the boys as well. The three of them were very close when they were children, and the other two haven't been the same since.

When Raymond was in the camp in Portsmouth he made friends with a lad who would drive them around. After we lost Raymond his friend came here for a trip to see the memorial and so on. There was a knock on the door and who answered it but his younger brother Ronnie. 'I know I've come to the right place,' he said straight away. Ronnie looked exactly like Raymond. And Raymond had described this place to the lad. 'He described it exactly as it is' he said. They were great friends.

ER

Raymond would come home as often as he could. I was thinking last night about him arriving on a Friday night and just throwing his case in. The whole family would know when Raymond was in the house. And bringing cigarettes for dad Tom. He never smoked cigarettes himself, but Taid would be delighted. And cigars for the boys. He would get them for next to nothing. We would hear the sound of that case for a long time afterwards.

TJR
Yes, he'd arrive on a Friday night. You'd expect him still every Friday night. He was popular with people, you know. The old people and everybody.

ER
His son, Paul, still lives in the village. We have just sent him a card for his 22nd birthday. He wasn't even two years old when he lost his father and he has no memories at all of him. He's exactly like Raymond and a lovely young man.

TJR
We've had dealings with Paul since his birth, and with his mother too. There are always two sides when a marriage breaks up, aren't there. We've given all of Raymond's things to Paul. We got a picture of the ship to give to him and Gray Thomas in Caernarfon framed it and refused to accept anything for doing that.

I don't want to see a war happening in Iraq (this was September 2002). That's not going to solve anything. It's fine for the boys who come back isn't it. But those who get killed, and their families - it's for them that it's bad.

I went to the Army myself in 1947, into the Royal Welsh Fusiliers first before being transferred to the North Staffordshire Regiment, and I was with the Internal Security in India before that. Six thousand were killed in Calcutta in

1946, and I was in the middle of those riots. That was extremely unpleasant work.

After I came back from India I went down to Lichfield Barracks and found myself in some Prisoner of War Hospital in Swindon. I became friends with one of the Germans. He was a Luftwaffe pilot and I've still got his photograph. He was only 19 and we became close friends. He was a conscript, - he'd had the call-up like me. Exactly the same as those boys on the *Belgrano*. I don't ever want to see another war.

ER
But wars there will be, won't there

TJR
Yes, I'm afraid so. As it says in the Bible, when will they ever learn.

GLOSSARY

Asado Argentinian barbecue.

Baqueano Title of 'guide' bestowed in recognition of his knowledge of the interior of Chubut on John D. Evans of Trevelin, who arrived originally on the *Mimosa* in 1865 aged 3. While leading an exploratory mission to establish a second Welsh settlement in the Andes, John Evans fled from an attack by a group of indigenous Mapuche which left three of his fellow Welsh pioneers dead. This was at Dyffryn y Merthyron ('Valley of the Martyrs'). Baqueano escaped through the subsequently renowned feat of his horse Malacara, which leapt a four metre ravine.

Calon Lân ('Pure Heart'). Classic Welsh hymn with a rousing crowd-pleasing chorus.

Canu penillion ('singing verses'). A form of Welsh folk music for voice and harp.

Carlo A familiar and less than respectful nickname for Charles, Prince of Wales. – first established in the song 'Carlo' (1969) by Welsh musician and activist Dafydd Iwan, which marked the Investiture of Charles, the English Prince of Wales. In Welsh usage, 'Carlo' is a diminutive of 'Charles', but more often used for a pet dog than a person.

Carn Fadryn A mountain on the Llŷn Peninsula. Madryn was the estate of Sir Thomas Love Jones-Parry who, with Lewis Jones, went to Buenos Aires in 1862 to negotiate with the Argentinian government the agreement for a Welsh settlement in Chubut. Puerto Madryn, near where the *Mimosa* landed in 1865, was named to honour this connection with Wales.

Cerdd dant ('string music'). Vocal improvisation over traditional Welsh melodies.

Chubut Valley ('Camwy' in Welsh). Site of the first Welsh settlement near to the landing place of the *Mimosa* in 1865. Including Puerto Madryn, Gaiman, Rawson, Trelew and Dolavon.

County Times Local newspaper published in Welshpool, Powys.

Cwm Hyfryd ('Beautiful Valley') New communities (Trevelin and Esquel) were established by one group of Welsh settlers who travelled four hundred miles across the Patagonian prairie and reached this fertile location in the foothills of the Andes in 1885.

Cynan The bardic name of Albert Evans-Jones, who wrote his poem 'Hwiangerddi' ('Lullabies'), mentioning Carn Fadryn, while on active service in Macedonia, Northern Greece, during World War 1.

Dôl y Plu ('Meadow of the Feathers'). The Welsh name for Las Plumas, located in Valle de los Mártires, Chubut.

Eisteddfod (plural 'eisteddfodau'). Welsh cultural festival of music, poetry and other literature, with a crowning and chairing of the bards who excel in different verse forms. The initial Chubut Eisteddfod took place some time within the first decade after the landing of the *Mimosa*.

Empire Games The multi-sport event which went by this name officially from 1930 to 1950 then became the British Empire and Commonwealth Games until 1974 when they were rebranded as the Commonwealth Games.

Gwladfa The Welsh settlement in Chubut, Patatgonia,

established with the *Mimosa* landing in 1865, where the language and culture could be maintained free from political and religious repression. Also **Y Wladfa** (adding the definite article 'Y').

Gwladfawyr People of Y Wladfa.

Hel Straeon ('Carrying Tales'). An **S4C** Welsh language TV magazine programme which ran from 1986 to 1997.

Hen Wlad The 'Old Country', Wales.

HTV The independent television company for Wales and the South West of England from 1970 to 2002.

Jones, Canon Alun Vicar of Llanberis, murdered by a 15 year old schoolboy in 1983.

Jones, Lewis Caernarfon born, one of the first group of settlers. Played a major role in the planning and construction of the railway connecting Puerto Madryn to the towns of the Chubut Valley.

Jones, Rev. Michael D. Welsh Congregationalist minister who anticipated Welsh nationalism in pursuing political means to protect Welsh identity and establish Welsh as the language of education, commerce, religion and government. He was a key figure in working towards establishing the settlement in Chubut as a means to achieve these ends.

Kelpers Nickname for Falklanders, whose islands are surrounded by giant kelp forests.

Llwyd ap Iwan Son of one of Y Wladfa's founding figures Michael D. Jones. A railway engineer, surveyor and explorer. Shot dead in 1909 by two North American bandits, Wilson and Evans.

Macedonia See **Cynan**.

Malacara See **Baqueano**.

MANWEB The former Merseyside and North Wales Electricty Board.

Mochyn Du Welsh comic song mourning the death of its title's eponymous black pig.

Mynydd Rhiw A small mountain on the Llŷn Peninsula.

Nain Welsh for 'grandmother'.

Nant y Pysgod ('Stream of the Fish'). Welsh name for Arroyo Pescado, near the cities of Esquel and Trevelin, where Llwyd ap Iwan was murdered by Wilson and Evans.

Rhyd yr Indiaid ('Indian Crossing'). The Welsh name for Paso de los Indios, a town in Cwn Hyfryd.

Y Dydd ('The Day') HTV's flagship Welsh language news programme.

Y Wladfa See **Gwladfa**.

Sudach chi ('How are you?'). This is among Horacio Kent's smatterings of Gwladfa Welsh, which also include 'bara menyn' (bread and butter) and 'teisen blât' (plate cake).

Paentio's Byd yn Wyrdd ('Painting the World Green'). Welsh popular song by Dafydd Iwan.

Sosban Fach ('Small Saucepan'). Traditional Welsh song of warmth, humour and enormous popularity. Also a rugby anthem of great note.

S4C Sianel Pedwar Cymru (Channel 4 Wales) launched in November 1982, Owes its existence in large part to the Welsh Nationalist Party leader Gwynfor Evans's threat of a hunger strike to force the British government to keep its promise to set up a Welsh language TV channel.

Taid Welsh for 'grandfather'.

Treorcki A town in the Chubut Valley between Gaiman and Trelew. Named after Treorchy in South Wales.

Tŷ Gwyn ('White House') Welsh tea house in Gaiman.

Urdd The Welsh League of Youth

Wish You Were Here A popular ITV holiday programme which ran in the UK from 1974 to 2003.

WOMBAT A recoilless anti-tank weapon.

Y Byd ar Bedwar ('The World on 4'). **S4C** documentary series broadcast from the launch of the channel in 1982.

Y Cymro Welsh language newspaper first published in 1932.

Y Dafarn Las ('The Blue Tavern') A pub in Gaiman.

Yma o Hyd Welsh popular song (1981) by Dafydd Iwan celebrating Welsh resilience and power to endure beyond the odds..

SOURCES
(2003 EDITION)

A full list of books and articles about Y Wladfa is available from the National Library of Wales: www.llgc.org.uk

The Guardian's material related to the war is among the fullest and most impartial archival collections available online. www.guardian.co.uk/Archive

The following books were useful for understanding the background.

THE WAR
Jimmy Burns, *The Land that Lost its Heroes* (Bloomsbury, 1987)
Max Hastings & Simon Jenkins, *The Battle for the Falklands* (Michael Joseph, 1983)
Martin Middlebrook, *The Falklands War* (Penguin, 1983)
The Sunday Times Insight Team, *The Falklands War* (Sphere Books, 1982)

ARGENTINA AND Y WLADFA
Bruce Chatwin, *In Patagonia* (Picador, 1977)
W. M. Hughes, *Ar Lannau's Gamwy* (Gwasg y Brython, 1927)
Joesph Seth Jones, *Dyddiau'r Mimosa*, ed. Elvey MacDonald (Gwasg Carreg Gwalch, 2002)
Elvey MacDonald, *Yr Hirdaith* (Gwasg Gomer, 1999)
Rough Guide Travel Guides, *The Rough Guide to Argentina*, (APA Publications, 2002)
Cathrin Williams, *Y Wladfa yn dy Boced* (Gwasg Pantycelyn, 2001)
R. Bryn Williams, *Y Wladfa* (Gwasg Prifysgol Cymru, 1962)

LANGUAGE

The interviews included in this book were conducted in Welsh, with the following exceptions.

In English: Bronwen Williams, Milton Rhys, Ronnie Gough and Denzil Connick

In Spanish: Carlos Eduardo Apiwan, Horatio Kent, Julio Oscar Gibbon and Celinde Espinoza de Austin. (Recorded *in situ* with Ioan Roberts and an interpreter then translated in full by Monica and Gwyn Jones)

SUPPLEMENTARY SOURCES
(2022 ENGLISH TRANSLATION)

Our selection is guided by *Rhyfel Ni*'s focus on individual experience and testimony rather than formal military history. We have also included a novel and a feature film which bring to life creatively themes in this book related to the war, Wales and Y Wladfa.

PREFACE

Darren Chetty, Grug Muse, Hanan Issa & Iestyn Tyne, *Welsh (Plural): Essays on the Future of Wales* (Repeater Books, 2022)

Fintan O'Toole *Heroic Failure: Brexit and the Politics of Pain* (Apollo, 2018)

Sathnam Sanghera *Empireland: How Imperialism Has Shaped Modern Britain* (Penguin, 2021)

Rebecca Solnit *Hope in the Dark: Untold Histories, Wild Possibilities* (Canongate, 2016)

THE WAR AND AFTER

High Bicheno *The Razor's Edge* (Orion, 2007)

Vincent Bramley, *Excursion to Hell* (Bloomsbury, 1991)

Daniel Kon *Los Chicos de la Guerra* (New English Library, 1983)

Paul Brown *Abandon Ship: the Real Story of the Sinkings in the Falklands War* (Osprey, 2021)

David Jackson *Surgeon in the Raw* (Mereo Books, 2020)

Larissa MacFarquhar 'An Ocean Apart: How Prosperity Transformed the Falklands' (*New Yorker*, 6th July 2020),

Hugh McManners *Forgotten Voices of the Falklands* (Ebury Press, 2008)

Ricky D Phillips *The First Casualty: The Untold Story of the Falklands War* (BEIC Books, 2019)

John Smith *74 Days: An Islander's Diary of the Falklands Occupation* (Cornerstone, 1984)

Edward Wilson *South Atlantic Requiem* (Arcadia, 2018)

Y WLADFA, ARGENTINA, WALES

http://www.cymru-ariannin.com/uploads/companion_to_the_welsh_settlement_in_patagonia.pdf

Marc Evans director *Patagonia* Welsh-Argentine feature film (Rainy Day Films, 2010)

Jon Gower *Gwalia Patagonia* (Gomer, 2015)

Geraldine Lublin *Memoir and Identity in Welsh Patagonia* (University of Wales Press, 2017)

Sergio Sepiurka & Jorge Miglioli *Rocky Trip: The Route of the Welsh in Patagonia* (Welsh Books Council, 2005)

Glyn Williams *The Desert and the Dream: A Study of Welsh Colonization in Chubut 1865-1915* (University of Wales Press, 1975)